ARE YOU A
MISERABLE
OLD GIT?

ARE YOU A MISERABLE OLD GIT?

Andrew John
and Stephen Blake

MICHAEL O'MARA BOOKS LIMITED

First published in Great Britain in 2006 by
Michael O'Mara Books Limited
9 Lion Yard, Tremadoc Road
London SW4 7NQ

A CIP catalogue record for this book is available
from the British Library

ISBN (10 digit): 1-84317-161-9
ISBN (13 digit): 978-1-84317-161-4

3 5 7 9 10 8 6 4

Designed and typeset by Martin Bristow

Printed and bound in Great Britain by Clays Ltd, St Ives plc

FOR MICKEY,
AT TIMES A SUPREMELY GROUCHY GIT,
AND THUS A GREAT INSPIRATION.

Contents

Contents

Contents

Acknowledgements

Who reads acknowledgements pages? Nobody we know. Have you ever seen a well-thumbed acknowledgements page? Thought not. So why bother? Oh, we might just mention our dear editor, Helen Cumberbatch, who has grizzled and griped at us to get our text in on time. No doubt she's gone through it with her accustomed high proficiency and meticulous scrutiny, so, if there are any problems or inaccuracies, you can blame her.

[9]

Introduction

We know what you're thinking: why write a book about being a miserable old git? Aren't there enough world-weary people around without encouraging more to crawl out of the woodwork? Well, if that is a genuine grouse on your part, join the club. You've just committed the ultimate grump: you've grumped about grumps. Congratulations! What do you want, a medal?

Are You a Miserable Old Git? takes a begrudging look at the world of the grouch, half-heartedly highlighting the many different sources of annoyance that are guaranteed to get the goat of moody moaners of all ages. Writing about miserable old gits tends to bring out the grumpiness in you, which is just as well for us as writers because it's enabled us to grumble about pet subjects of our own: kids, animals, entertainment, media, politicians, technology – all the usual suspects. We've also included quotes and insights from a range of celebrated individuals: from art and literature – Francis Bacon, Oscar Wilde, Bertolt Brecht, Charles Baudelaire, Samuel Beckett; from politics – Winston Churchill, Benjamin Disraeli; from the world of cinema – Woody Allen, Groucho Marx, W. C. Fields; to name but a few.

These wonderful people have, over the years, redressed the balance and stopped cheery, air-headed, happy-clappy, optimistic halfwits from having it all their own way and making us think this wretched world is any better than it is. They have stood up, flown the flag, let themselves be counted and used their art for the sake of grumpiness and malcontentedness – and long may their works live on.

Essentially, this unashamed misery-fest of a book amply provides you with all kinds of things about which to be grumpy, as well as giving insights into the psyche of a miserable old git. If you're a bona fide grump, you'll agree with every word we say (although it'll be obvious that *some* of it is written with tongues firmly in cheeks and should be taken in the appropriate spirit).

So, as you can see, we've done our best in truly trying circumstances. We did tell our publishers we wouldn't actually *enjoy* putting together this cheerless, dismal little volume, that it would be far better if we just went into a corner and griped about how appalling things are – or just quietly withered. They didn't respond.

And we were right. It's been a depressing slog from beginning to end and, quite frankly, you're welcome to it! In fact, we hope it makes you thoroughly cat-kickingly cantankerous, not to mention peevish, petulant and down-right irritable. *We're* off to the pub to complain about the beer and put the world to rights with all the other miserable old gits.

ANDREW JOHN and STEPHEN BLAKE
March 2006

Don't Talk to Me About Life, or Why we get miserable and moody about things in general

'Life always comes to a bad end.'
MARCEL AYMÉ, French writer

Admit it: you love to have a moan; you savour the daily gripe; you look forward to a good old grouse. Let's face it: everybody's at it these days because there's so much to be miserable about! It's become the norm. How can we be happy about *anything* in this mad, mad world of ours?

For our part, we find plenty of things to be miserable about:

- technology that's supposed to make your life easier and save you time, and does neither;

- politicians who want to collect all our personal details and sell them to megabucks corporations so they can target us in their marketing campaigns and try to sell us things no one with even the sanity of a brain-damaged wombat would want to buy – and all in the cause of foisting unwanted ID cards on us;

- the most powerful man on Planet Earth with his finger hovering over the nuclear button, who famously (or infamously) thinks that the French don't have a word for 'entrepreneur' and once made an astonishing enquiry about which 'state' Wales was in;

[13]

- the way the National Health Service loses too many of its patients to virulent hospital bugs;

- bleating religionists of the Really Serious variety who go whingeing to the newspapers if someone so much as *suggests* that their chosen faith, sect or cult might be just a tad intolerant;

- millions of channels of total garbage on television;

- trains that don't arrive on time – if they run at all;

- millions *more* channels of total garbage on television;

- bad grammar on the B bloody B bloody C – right where it *shouldn't* be . . .

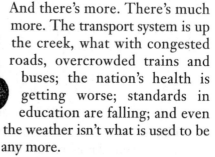

And there's more. There's much more. The transport system is up the creek, what with congested roads, overcrowded trains and buses; the nation's health is getting worse; standards in education are falling; and even the weather isn't what is used to be any more.

But don't get us started! We could go on for ever about life and the miseries it holds in store. Thankfully, there are several people – and a fictional robot – who have at times felt downright grouchy enough to do it for us, and, in the interests of spreading a bit of crabbiness about, we bring you some of their grouchier moments . . .

Quotable Querulous Quibbles About Life

He who laughs has not yet heard the bad news.
BERTOLT BRECHT,
German poet and playwright

∗

Broadly speaking, human beings may be divided
into three classes: those who are billed to death,
those who are worried to death and those
who are bored to death.
WINSTON CHURCHILL,
British Prime Minister

∗

For every complex problem, there is a solution
that is simple, neat and wrong.
H. L. MENCKEN,
US journalist, critic and editor

∗

I know of no existing nation that deserves to live.
And I know of very few individuals.
H. L. MENCKEN

∗

The older I get the more I admire and crave competence,
just simple competence, in any field from adultery
to zoology.
H. L. MENCKEN

What good is a long life to us if it is hard,
joyless and so full of suffering that we can only
welcome death as a deliverer?
SIGMUND FREUD, Austrian physician
and founder of psychoanalysis

*

'It's snowing still,' said Eeyore gloomily.
'So it is.'
'*And* freezing.'
'Is it?'
'Yes,' said Eeyore. 'However,' he said, brightening up a
little, 'we haven't had an earthquake recently.'
A. A. MILNE, British author
(from *Winnie-the-Pooh*)

*

'Good morning, Little Piglet,' said Eeyore. 'If it is a good
morning,' he said. 'Which I doubt,' said he. 'Not that it
matters,' he said.
A. A. MILNE
(from *Winnie-the-Pooh*)

Don't Talk to Me About Life

Life? Don't talk to me about life.

Life, loathe it or ignore it, you can't like it.

Do you want me to sit in a corner and rust or just fall
apart where I'm standing?

Don't pretend you want to talk to me,
I know you hate me.

I only have to talk to somebody and they begin to hate
me. Even robots hate me. If you just ignore me I expect
I shall probably go away.

Here I am, brain the size of a planet, and they ask me to
take you to the bridge. Call that job satisfaction? I don't.

Sorry, did I say something wrong? Pardon me for
breathing, which I never do anyway so I don't know why
I bother to say it; oh, God, I'm so depressed.

Don't feel you have to take any notice of me, please.

Marvin the Paranoid Android,
in Douglas Adams's *The Hitchhiker's Guide
to the Galaxy* and its sequels

*

Starbucks makes pretty good coffee. That's got to
be a good thing. But it's all those newspapers
and 'Hey, wow' sofas, and the *pain au raisin*
that goes with it that I can't stand.
Bob Geldof, Irish rock musician,
and Live Aid and Live 8 organizer

Are You a Miserable Old Git?

My band call me Victor Meldrew. My kids call me
Victor Meldrew. I actually think that when my hair finally
falls out I'll find that I probably am Victor Meldrew.
RICK WAKEMAN, British musician
(Victor Meldrew was the grumpy main character
played by Richard Wilson in the British TV sitcom
One Foot in the Grave)

*

Of course it's possible to love a human being
if you don't know them too well.
CHARLES BUKOWSKI, US poet and author

*

To the discontented man no chair is easy.
BENJAMIN FRANKLIN, US author,
diplomat, philosopher and scientist

At the ominous word 'liberality',
Scrooge frowned and shook his head.
CHARLES DICKENS, British novelist
(from *A Christmas Carol*)

If it's good, they'll stop making it.
Herbert Block,
US political cartoonist

*

Idealism is fine, but as it approaches reality the cost
becomes prohibitive.
William F. Buckley Jnr,
US author and commentator

*

I just dress in what is comfortable and covers up my gut
as much as possible, because the problem is that
I look like a minicab driver. You know, there are some
of us that are just fated to look like a minicab driver.
It doesn't matter what clothes you put on, or how
much you pay for them, you're still going to look
like a minicab driver.
John Peel,
British radio DJ and presenter

*

The world is so dreadfully managed,
one hardly knows to whom to complain.
Ronald Firbank, British writer

*

Those who have some means think that
the most important thing in the world is love.
The poor know that it is money.
Gerald Brenan, British essayist

A conference is a gathering of important people
who singly can do nothing, but together can decide
that nothing can be done.
FRED ALLEN, US comedian

*

WINSTON CHURCHILL, visiting Niagara Falls for the
second time, was asked to his obvious irritation whether
the falls looked the same as when, decades earlier, he had
first seen them. 'Well,' he growled, 'the principle seems
the same. The water keeps falling over.'

*

I have neither the scholar's melancholy, which is
emulation; nor the musician's, which is fantastical; nor
the courtier's, which is proud; nor the soldier's, which is
ambitious; nor the lawyer's, which is politic; nor the
lady's, which is nice; nor the lover's, which is all these:
but it is a melancholy of mine own, compounded of many
simples, extracted from many objects, and indeed the
sundry contemplation of my travels, in which my often
rumination wraps me in a most humorous sadness.
WILLIAM SHAKESPEARE, British playwright
(spoken by Jaques in *As You Like It*,
Act IV, Scene I)

*

Past and to come seems best; things present worst.
WILLIAM SHAKESPEARE
(spoken by the Archbishop
in *King Henry the Fourth, Part II*,
Act I, Scene III)

Don't Talk to Me About Life

I don't want to achieve immortality through my work:
I want to achieve it through not dying.
Woody Allen, US film director
and screenwriter

*

More than any other time in history, mankind faces
a crossroads. One path leads to despair and utter
hopelessness, the other to total extinction.
Let us pray we have the wisdom to choose correctly.
Woody Allen (in *Side Effects*)

*

It seemed the world was divided into good and bad
people. The good ones slept better . . . while the bad ones
seemed to enjoy the waking hours much more.
Woody Allen (in *Side Effects*)

*

Life is divided into the horrible and the miserable.
Woody Allen (in *Annie Hall*)

*

Life is a concentration camp. You're stuck here and
there's no way out, and you can only rage impotently
against your persecutors.
Woody Allen

*

It's not that I'm afraid to die.
I just don't want to be there when it happens.
Woody Allen

Are You a Miserable Old Git?

Remember that as a teenager you are in the last stage
of your life when you will be happy to hear
that the phone is for you.
FRAN LEBOWITZ, US journalist

*

People (a group that in my opinion has always attracted
an undue amount of attention) have often been likened to
snowflakes. This analogy is meant to suggest that each is
unique – no two alike. This is quite patently not the case.
People . . . are quite simply a dime a dozen. And, I hasten
to add, their only similarity to snowflakes resides in
their invariable and lamentable tendency to turn,
after a few warm days, to slush.
FRAN LEBOWITZ

*

They f**k you up, your mum and dad . . .
PHILIP LARKIN, British poet (from 'This Be The Verse')

*

Ha! Easy for nuns to talk about giving up things.
That's what they do for a living.
GARRISON KEILLOR, US writer and broadcaster

*

Experience is a good teacher, but she sends in terrific bills.
MINNA ANTRIM, US writer

*

'Modern Life Is Rubbish'
BLUR, song and album title

Good morning – *stupid*.
LUDWIG VAN BEETHOVEN,
German composer (greeting an assistant)

*

The G in AGA syndrome stands for Grumpiness,
midway between the A for Anger that you feel
when you are young, and the A for Acquiescence
you feel when you realize it's all gone to hell
and there is nothing you can do about it.
STUART PREBBLE, executive producer
and writer of the BBC series *Grumpy Old Men*

*

The average man's opinions are much less foolish
than they would be if he thought for himself.
BERTRAND RUSSELL,
British philosopher and mathematician

A market is a place set apart for men to deceive
and get the better of one another.
ANACHARSIS,
Greek philosopher (sixth century BCE)

*

If you want to annoy your neighbours,
tell the truth about them.
PIETRO ARETINO, Italian satirist

*

What passes for optimism is most often the effect of an
intellectual error.
RAYMOND ARON, French political thinker

*

People seem to enjoy things more when they know a lot
of other people have been left out on the pleasure.
RUSSELL BAKER, US humorist

*

Inanimate objects are classified scientifically into three
major categories – those that don't work, those that break
down and those that get lost.
RUSSELL BAKER

*

I don't know what is worse: old men moaning, or people
moaning about old men moaning, or people moaning
about moaners moaning about moaning . . . Modern life
is full of opportunities, make the most of it!
DAN, contributor to a BBC website

Nothing matters very much,
and few things matter at all.
Arthur James Balfour,
British Prime Minister (attributed)

*

If you would know what the Lord God thinks of money,
you have only to look at those to whom he gives it.
Maurice Baring,
British novelist and critic

*

What we call 'progress' is the exchange
of one nuisance for another nuisance.
Havelock Ellis, British sexologist

*

A great many people think they are thinking
when they are merely rearranging their prejudices.
William James, US philosopher

Are You a Miserable Old Git?

Life is a hospital in which every patient
is possessed by the desire to change his bed.
CHARLES BAUDELAIRE, French poet

*

The reason we drive motor cars is that, once we've got
one, we're free. But the conflict between that idealism
and the reality that you get in your motor car is that
you're exposed not to freedom, opportunities, discovery,
delight – you're exposed to frustration, dirt, danger
and aggression, and that's what makes us so cross.
That, I believe, is the source of road rage.
STEPHEN BAYLEY, British writer,
critic and style guru

*

I've had hypnotherapy, acupuncture, people hitting me
with twigs. I had another man who electrocuted me every
time I had a fag. That didn't stop me. Oh, dear, it's a
terrible thing. Grumpy old man? This is my sixth day
without a cigarette and I could rip your f***ing head off.
ARTHUR SMITH, British writer and comedian

*

Why did nature create Man? Was it to show that she is
big enough to make mistakes, or was it pure ignorance?
HOLBROOK JACKSON, British journalist and writer

*

One has to look out for engineers – they begin with
sewing machines and end up with the atomic bomb.
MARCEL PAGNOL, French playwright

Rantings of a Miserable Old Git: Part I

There are some things you read in newspapers, hear on the radio or watch on TV that have obviously been deliberately chosen to stimulate the crabby and cantankerous components of your autonomic nervous system; items that have been put there just to get people going. Here's a selection of the kind of stuff that makes you want to screw up the paper you read them in and throw it at the radio or TV that you heard them on.

- In a BBC poll, 5 per cent of the 15–34-year-olds questioned thought that Gandalf was the mastermind behind the defeat of the Spanish Armada. Of this sorry sample of the population, about 33 per cent didn't know that the Battle of Britain occurred during the Second World War. What is education for, exactly?

- George W. Bush once asked the Welsh singer Charlotte Church which state Wales was in. (In a better state than America, no doubt.)

- The antidepressant drug with the generic name of paroxetine was raising concern in August 2005 because, according to scientists in Oslo, far from relieving depression it was causing people to become suicidal. Well, opting to top oneself is definitely one way to cure one's depression.

- According to figures from Richard Bacon, MP, chairman of the Public Accounts Committee (at the time of writing), £100 million is spent each year in the UK on training teachers who end up never teaching. The same figures reveal that an IT project for the probation service had seven managers in seven years, and five of them didn't know anything about project management. The project went 70 per cent over budget. Aren't you glad your taxes paid for this?

- The sales of anti-sickness pills have doubtless shot up in the UK since the BBC changed its TV weather maps. Now you feel like throwing up as you're hurled at three times the speed of sound from Land's End to John O'Groats and sometimes back again – all within about twenty seconds. What was wrong with Michael Fish and his magnetic clouds? Then again, the colour of his jackets didn't exactly aid digestion either . . .

- You get a fault on your line and ring the phone company. Their maddening, merry-go-round menu system has you jabbing at keys till your fingertips bleed and you eventually find yourself trying to explain the problem to a spotty sixteen-year-old 'adviser' whose communications skills are only marginally superior to those of an adolescent chimp. After it becomes painfully obvious that you'd be better off climbing up the telegraph pole and fixing the fault yourself, your rage has become so extreme it could power the national grid. Eventually the telecom employee gives you a number to ring, and when you put the phone down to dial the number he grunted at you, it's only when you're halfway through the menu system that you realize it's the same number you rang three-quarters of an hour ago. After dunking your head in a bowl of icy water and knocking back several stiff drinks, you contact a rival phone company and have your account transferred. That'll show the bastards.

White Heat and Snake Oil,
or Why technology is so often
a load of crap

'The thing with high-tech is that you always
end up using scissors.'
DAVID HOCKNEY, British artist

That Harold Wilson geezer who used to run the country
in the 1960s and 1970s never did say 'white heat of
technology'. He's been misquoted ever since thanks to
stupid people who haven't bothered to check the facts. To
set the record straight, what that Labour Prime Minister
did say was this: 'We are redefining and we are restating
our socialism in terms of the scientific revolution . . . the
Britain that is going to be forged in the white heat of this
revolution will be no place for restrictive practices or
outdated methods on either side of industry.' So there.

But look what that comment unleashed. All the labour-
saving gizmos that were supposed to give us all the
freedom not to work? Hardly – we're all working harder
than ever. What we did end up with, though, were a host
of utterly useless creations that do more to antagonize
than to help us cope with the daily grind:

- mobile phones with infuriating ringtones that sound
  like frogs on crack;

- the opportunity to speak to a call-centre operative
  in Mumbai to find out the size of our unauthorized

overdraft at our bank, whose local branch was just down the road till they transferred it to the other end of the country and merged it with a sock manufacturer;

- instruction booklets written in Klingon by Martians who failed their GCSE in intergalactic languages;

- silicon snake oil in the form of gadgets you never knew you wanted until you were told you couldn't do without them.

We've now got more TV channels than you can shake a digibox at, all offering total crap, thereby proving that choice and quality are inversely proportional to each other. We have mobile phones with cameras that have enabled juvenile thugs to go around filming attacks on total strangers and sending the images to their equally reprobate friends.

Doesn't it make you grumpy when ...

... you've been slaving over a hot computer for an hour, but you forget to save or back up your files so that when the system suddenly crashes, you end up losing all your precious work? Though it may be possible to retrieve the lost data with the help of experts, you know it'll be quicker (and a lot cheaper) to begin from scratch, even though the mere thought of it brings you out in a cold sweat.

We all know what it's like when an item of apparently advanced technology fails to deliver the goods; when it suddenly stops doing what it's supposed to be doing; when batteries fail after only a few uses; when mobile phones stop accepting calls, digital cameras stop taking pictures, and DVD players stop playing DVDs. Worst of all is when you're trying to figure out why something won't work and you have to wade through a three-inch-thick manual printed on third-rate bog roll in pidgin English. After ten minutes it's obvious you're getting nowhere fast, and you'd probably be better off reading it in French.

Vorsprung durch Technik (German for 'progress through technology')? Get real!

Such a despairing attitude among users of 'modern' technology is far from unique in this day and age, as quite a few other people are less than blissful about the so-called technological revolution, too ...

Quotable Querulous Quibbles About Technology

The biggest lie that the technology manufacturers sell
you is 'Plug and go'. It's 'plug and "F**k me, I don't know
what's going on here"', and it's hours and hours.
'What are you doing in there?' from the kitchen.
'I've just bought a new piece of kit, darling,
and I'm just sorting it out.' And it goes on for weeks,
you know. 'Plug and go'? It's a joke.
MICHAEL GRADE, Chairman of the BBC

To err is human, but to really foul things up
requires a computer.
PHILIP HOWARD, British journalist and author

*

Computers are anti-Faraday machines. He [Faraday]
said he couldn't understand anything until he could
count it, while computers count everything and
understand nothing.
RALPH CORNES, *The Guardian*

*

One machine can do the work of fifty ordinary men.
No machine can do the work of one extraordinary man.
ELBERT HUBBARD, US writer, printer and editor

If you put tomfoolery into a computer, nothing comes out but tomfoolery. But this tomfoolery, having passed through a very expensive machine, is somehow ennobled and no one dares criticize it.
Pierre Gallois, French scientist

*

Machines are worshipped because they are beautiful, and valued because they confer power; they are hated because they are hideous, and loathed because they impose slavery.
Bertrand Russell, British philosopher

*

Mechanics, not microbes, are the menace to civilization.
Norman Douglas, British writer

One servant is worth a thousand gadgets.
Joseph Alois Schumpeter,
US economist and social theorist

White Heat and Snake Oil

Technology . . . the knack of so arranging the world
that we need not experience it.
Max Frisch, Swiss playwright

*

A modern computer hovers between the obsolescent
and the nonexistent.
Sydney Brenner, British scientist

*

If the human race wants to go to hell in a basket,
technology can help it get there by jet.
Charles M. Allen, US scientist

The unleashed power of the atom has changed everything
save our modes of thinking and we thus drift toward
unparalleled catastrophe.
Albert Einstein, German mathematician

*

It has become appallingly obvious that our technology
has exceeded our humanity.
Albert Einstein

Science and technology multiply around us.
To an increasing extent they dictate the languages
in which we speak and think. Either we use those
languages, or we remain mute.
J. G. BALLARD,
British writer

*

Technology causes problems as well as solves problems.
Nobody has figured out a way to ensure that,
as of tomorrow, technology won't create problems.
Technology simply means increased power, which is
why we have the global problems we face today.
JARED DIAMOND,
US physiologist

*

No crash-proof [computer] system can be built
unless it is made for an idiot.
ELLEN ULLMAN, US writer

White Heat and Snake Oil

As we push our technologies to exploit more and more resources, we now recognize that both the direct devastation and the unforeseen consequences are becoming increasingly global in nature.
RICHARD NORGAARD,
US writer

*

The ethic of progress – in effect, the ethic of perpetual technospheric expansion – is in reality no more than an ethic of biospheric destruction . . .
it is an anti-evolutionary ethic.
EDWARD GOLDSMITH,
British ecologist and business executive

*

Sirs, I have tested your machine. It adds a new terror to life and makes death a long-felt want.
HERBERT BEERBOHM TREE,
British actor and theatrical impresario,
referring to a gramophone (attributed)

The telephone is a good way to talk to people
without having to offer them a drink.
FRAN LEBOWITZ, US journalist

*

In these days of computer viruses, asking if you
may put your disk into someone's computer
is the technological equivalent of unsafe sex.
RUTH DUDLEY EDWARDS,
Irish historian, writer and journalist

*

I've heard that myth quite seriously expressed . . .
that the beast in the Book of Revelation
will be a monster computer.
BILL ELLIS,
British specialist in modern folklore

The Science of Being a Grump, or Why it's perfectly normal to be a miserable old git

'Oh, wouldn't the world seem dull and flat
With nothing whatever to grumble at?'
W. S. GILBERT, British dramatist and librettist

Believe it or not, scientists at Vanderbilt University in Nashville, Tennessee, recently discovered that some people are naturally predisposed to having a grumpy outlook on life simply because they're born that way – it's in their genes.

In 2002, psychologist Dr David Zald identified a small area of the brain that he believes controls people's tendency to have frequent attacks of anger, irritability or anxiety.

The more active that section of the brain, the more likely a person will suffer from bad moods and general grumpiness.

According to Zald: 'It looks like it is this part of the brain's activity that regulates people's mood. It is also a part of the brain that controls sweating, stomach acidity and heart rate, and other physical feelings associated with stress and bad moods.'

This particular part of the human brain, which is no bigger than a postage stamp, is called the ventromedial prefrontal cortex; it lies an inch or two behind the right eye. Zald used eighty-nine people in his study, and scanned their brains using a technique known as positron emission tomography, or PET. These men and women were then asked to complete a detailed survey of their state of mind over the last month. Those who experienced many bad moods were also revealed to have a lot of extra activity in the ventromedial prefrontal cortex.

Zald's research is backed up by studies on people who have suffered damage in that area of the brain, who often lose the ability to feel angst or stress. 'They could literally think to themselves: "Should I bet that $10,000 on a roll of the dice?" and not feel anything in the pit of their stomach. They just don't feel anxiety, which is linked to bad moods,' said Zald.

So there you have it – the perfect excuse to justify being a miserable old git!

**Signs to look out for if you think you might
have turned into a miserable old git:**

- when you get home from from work or from a shopping spree you've got at least three gripes to share with your partner or family . . .

- you whinge at every opportunity;

- tuts and heavy sighs punctuate your conversations with disturbing frequency;

- you generally see the worst in every situation;

- any moments of happiness you experience are few and short-lived;

- you realize you've not smiled or laughed in weeks.

All Creatures Great and Vile, or Why do animals get right up your nose?

'God in his wisdom made the fly
And then forgot to tell us why.'
OGDEN NASH, US poet and humorist

*

What is it that gives all dogs, no matter what their breed, licence to sniff at one's crotch? And why do they always do it in front of an audience? Is it simply to maximize embarrassment, perhaps?

It's always the same: you're trying to be polite during a chance encounter with a dog-owning neighbour, and, before you can take evasive action, the bothersome beast is coming at you at 90 miles an hour before burying his nose in your groin, and sniffing and grunting loudly. In spite of your obvious discomfort, rather than drag the annoying mutt away from you, the neighbour invariably gazes fondly at her dear little bundle of fur, remarking on his playful nature and assuring you that he is 'just being friendly'. Occasionally, when your plight has been ignored for too long, it becomes necessary to take matters into your own hands: deploying a subtle little kick (in the direction of the beast, not its owner) can often be used to good effect. 'Funny,' you say above the high-pitched yelping, 'something seems to have spooked the little fella.'

Dogs also have fleas – nasty, germ-carrying creatures that any self-respecting creator should have thought twice about inflicting upon the earth. With about 1,600 species of flea in existence across the globe, the world's entire flea population probably weighs more than that of the world's humans. If your dog has fleas, although there may be only a couple of dozen on the creature, there will be another 10,000 on the carpet waiting to jump on your warm-blooded body to hitch a ride elsewhere.

Cats carry fleas, too. While a dog will at least pretend to be your friend, a cat has an icy contempt for anything but itself, and you know damned well that the only reason it stays with you is because you give it food. If it jumps into your lap it's simply because it senses that you're more comfortable than the floor. It hates you. You're just a convenient bed with a bolt-on feeding facility.

And when it brings a pathetic little bunch of blood and feathers that was once a living, vibrant, melodious little bird, *and gives it to you as a present*, it's disgusting.

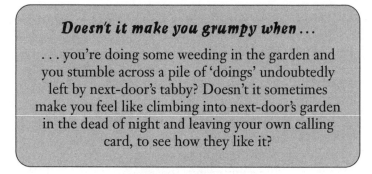

Doesn't it make you grumpy when ...

... you're doing some weeding in the garden and you stumble across a pile of 'doings' undoubtedly left by next-door's tabby? Doesn't it sometimes make you feel like climbing into next-door's garden in the dead of night and leaving your own calling card, to see how they like it?

And what about those furry little things like gerbils, guinea pigs, rabbits and hamsters. What do you *do* with a hamster, for goodness' sake?

Many people seem to have a pet mentality combined with an anthropomorphic view of pets: 'Oh, they're so cute and wouldn't hurt a fly [they'd be more useful if they did] and *ever* so intelligent, you know.' Yeah, they're clever enough to know that the disgusting brown mush you've just spooned out of the can is food, and that if they pretend to show you unconditional love and affection they'll be fed and taken care of until their dying day.

We're obviously not alone in maintaining a healthy distrust of these four-legged fiends, as this selection of opinions clearly shows.

Quotable Querulous Quibbles About Creatures

People who hate children and small dogs can't be all bad.
W. C. FIELDS, US actor and comedian

*

The rabbit has a charming face;
Its private life is a disgrace.
I really dare not name to you
The awful things that rabbits do . . .
ANONYMOUS (1925)

To my mind, the only possible pet is a cow.
Cows love you . . . They will listen to your problems
and never ask a thing in return. They will be your friends
for ever. And, when you get tired of them, you can kill
and eat them. Perfect.
BILL BRYSON, US writer

*

The trouble with a kitten is that
When it grows up it's always a cat.
OGDEN NASH

Are You a Miserable Old Git?

Cats are bastards . . . If cats could find a way to push
all the people in the world into an active volcano and still
open all the tins of catfood, they would . . . Cats are,
in short, the scum of the earth.
DAVID QUANTICK, British comedian and writer

∗

And as for those old women who have nothing better to
do than go out and spread the contents of their breadbins
all over your local green space so that pigeons will come
along and empty their bowels over everything and
everyone – wouldn't you just love to see one of those
old dears feeding the pigeons one sunny morning
and suddenly an unmarked van screech up, the doors
fly open and four masked men leap out, throw her
in the back and she's never seen again?
DAVID QUANTICK

∗

(There are) more ways of killing a cat
than choking her with cream.
CHARLES KINGSLEY, British novelist and cleric

∗

Cats seem to go on the principle that it never does
any harm to ask for what you want.
JOSEPH WOOD KRUTCH, US essayist and naturalist

∗

Laboratory guinea pigs say to themselves:
'I bet they would not do that to polar bears.'
RAMÓN GÓMEZ DE LA SERNA, Spanish novelist

The old grey donkey, Eeyore, stood by himself in a thistly
corner of the Forest, his front feet well apart, his head
on one side, and thought about things. Sometimes he
thought sadly to himself, 'Why?' and sometimes
he thought, 'Wherefore?' and sometimes he thought,
'Inasmuch as which?' and sometimes he didn't quite
know what he was thinking about.
A. A. MILNE, British author
(from *Winnie-the-Pooh*)

*

You know, I have never deliberately run over a fox.
They are always too quick for me. But dogs.
I don't like dogs. Because owners always assume
you like their dogs as much as they do.
RORY McGRATH, British comedian

*

Cats are autocrats of naked self-interest.
They are both amoral and immoral, consciously
breaking rules . . . the cat may be the only animal
who savours the perverse or reflects upon it.
CAMILLE PAGLIA, US academic and author

[47]

Songs for the Sad, Music for the Miserable

'Heaven Knows I'm Miserable Now' – THE SMITHS

'Why Does It Always Rain On Me?' – TRAVIS

'Prayers For Rain' – THE CURE

'I Hate Myself And Want To Die' – NIRVANA

'Without You' – MARIAH CAREY

'Girlfriend In A Coma' – THE SMITHS

'Happy Being Miserable' – LENINGRAD COWBOYS

'Ain't No Sunshine' – BILL WITHERS

'Misery' – SOUL ASYLUM

'I Don't Like Mondays' – THE BOOMTOWN RATS

'Rainy Days And Mondays (Always Get Me Down)' – THE CARPENTERS

'Mardy Bum' – ARCTIC MONKEYS

'(I) Love To Hate You' – ERASURE

The Medium is the Massage, or Why we are not amused by TV and other attempts to divert and inform us

'In California they don't throw their garbage away –
they make it into television shows.'
Woody Allen, US film director and screenwriter

TV today is undoubtedly a shadow of its former self, particularly now that there is barely anything on the small screen of any real value. Take 'reality TV' shows, such as *Big Brother*, as a case in point. A bunch of fame-hungry losers are put in a specially constructed house and told to act 'normal'. For weeks on end the viewing public watches these saddos uttering the most boring and inane crap, and, while the most annoying people get evicted, others stay in. The winner becomes an instant celebrity . . . for about fifteen nanoseconds, and then they're forgotten because *Slightly Well-Known People Watch Paint Dry While Playing With Their Private Parts* has just begun on ITV.

Then there are those programmes whose sole aim is to make you throw up into your TV dinner. There was *Nip and Tuck*, a reality show that gleefully encouraged you to witness flabby, spoiled, loaded pillocks having bits removed, sewn up, pulled a bit this way and a bit that way, stretched, loosened and sucked out. Yuck! This is not to be confused with the similarly titled *Nip/Tuck*, a US drama series that gleefully encouraged you to witness flabby, spoiled, loaded pillocks having bits removed, sewn up, pulled a bit this way and a bit that way, stretched, loosened and sucked out.

> ### *Doesn't it make you grumpy when ...*
>
> . . . you're watching TV at dinner time, when, in the middle of an ad break, you're confronted with an advert about cream to cure piles, or a commercial about tampons, thrush or incontinence pads? Surely such ads could be confined to broadcast slots when viewers are less likely to be put off their lunchtime snack or evening meal.

'Sixteen channels of shit,' sang Pink Floyd on their album *The Wall*. How right they were . . . You can get digiboxes now, or one of those weird-shaped woks that decorate virtually every house in the known universe, which bring not sixteen but *sixty* channels of it. And then some.

Then there are twenty-four-hour news channels, which have so much information plastered all over the screen that you can't possibly take it all in at once. And half the screen is always covered with vast areas of garish colour that do nothing more than obscure vital bits of the pictures of the current news story with scrolling text. It's pure information overload. And what about the annoying little icons in the top-left corner of the digital channels that tell you that you're tuned to BBC3 or ITV2? Surely every viewer knows which channel they're watching because they chose it in the first place . . . Give the viewing public *some* credit, please!

Grumps of Page and Screen

Before we leave entertainment, writers and media in general, we ought to pay honourable tribute to a few notable grumps who have brought a little reassuringly depressing gloom and despondency to our lives.

ALF GARNETT

There were few TV characters better known for grumping and grousing about everything than Alf Garnett, played by Warren Mitchell. No greater malcontent was there than he – except perhaps the curmudgeonly Victor Meldrew.

Till Death Us Do Part, which introduced crotchety Alf to the world, was a seminal sixties sitcom written by Johnny Speight that paved the way for many like it. Alf wasn't Speight's first grumpy character, however: some years before *Till Death Us Do Part*, he had developed *The Arthur Haynes Show*, whose 'hero' was a chip-on-the-shoulder socialist of whom Alf Garnett was a right-wing mirror – monarchist, Tory-voting, racist bigot extraordinaire, with a loud mouth and a foul temper to match.

Garnett was called Alf Ramsey in the pilot episode, but the name was changed in deference to the England football manager who took his team to World Cup victory soon after the first series of *Till Death Us Do Part* began.

VICTOR MELDREW

A much later malcontent was, of course, Victor Meldrew, played by the actor and director Richard Wilson, OBE, Rector of the University of Glasgow (1996–9) and an associate member of RADA, in David Renwick's comedy series *One Foot in the Grave*.

Renowned for the unforgettable catchphrase, 'I don't *believe* it!' Wilson was fifty-three when he began life as Meldrew, and Victor was sixty. At first, Wilson turned down the part because he thought he was too young. 'I suppose I hadn't really thought of myself as playing older people and I was surprised to be asked,' he is quoted as saying.

MARVIN THE PARANOID ANDROID

One of the best-loved grumps isn't human at all – neither a fictional human character nor a real person. He's a robot – Marvin the so-called 'paranoid android' – that was probably more depressed than paranoid, and one of the principal characters in Douglas Adams's popular science-fiction series *The Hitchhiker's Guide to the Galaxy*.

Adams has said that Marvin is part of a long line of literary depressives, such as A. A. Milne's Eeyore and Jaques in Shakespeare's *As You Like It* (both quoted in these pages), and even owes something to the author's own periods of depression.

Marvin's grumpiness and melancholy are demonstrated in a telling passage from the book series:

> 'I got very bored and depressed, so I went and plugged myself into [the ship's] external computer feed. I talked to the computer at great length, and explained my view of the universe to it,' said Marvin.
>
> 'And what happened?' pressed Ford [Prefect].
>
> 'It committed suicide,' said Marvin.

The character of Marvin appears to have been inspired by a comedy writer by the name of Andrew Marshall, with whom Adams was acquainted. An insight into the former's disposition is provided by Adams in his Foreword to *The Hitchhiker's Guide to the Galaxy: The Original Radio Scripts*, describing the scene after Marshall had said something rude to someone in a pub:

> In the silence that followed Andrew would then wander off into a corner and sit hunched over a pint of beer. I would go over and say, 'Andrew, what on earth was the point of saying that?' and Andrew would say, 'What's the point of not saying it? What's the point of being here? What's the point of anything? Including being alive at all? That seems particularly pointless to me.'

No wonder he was an inspiration for Marvin!

W. C. Fields

Also much quoted in these pages – because we think his acerbic wit is so funny and often so close to the truth – is W. C. Fields (1880–1946), born William Claude Dukenfield in Philadelphia, Pennsylvania, USA.

This stocky, bulbous-nosed, leathery-faced figure with the gravelly voice was a juggler at the start of his professional life, and did the variety circuits throughout the USA, South Africa and Europe. Fields starred in several silent films, and didn't disabuse his fans of the idea that he was a curmudgeon off-screen as well as on.

DOROTHY PARKER

Another favourite American wit is Dorothy Parker (1893–1967), famed for that razor-sharp *mot juste*. She was born in New Jersey, and was a drama critic for *Vanity Fair* and *Vogue*. She wrote reviews, short stories and sketches – and of course poems – all vehicles for her sardonic humour.

AMBROSE BIERCE

Compiler of the wonderful work *The Devil's Dictionary* (1911), Ambrose Bierce (1842–*c*.1914) is another American favourite of ours.

Bierce sharpened his political wit by becoming a political journalist. After the American Civil War, he wrote satirical political pieces for the *News-Letter*, which he eventually edited. After moving to London he began writing caustic material for *Figaro* and *Fun* magazines under the name of Dod Grile. A fascination with death and horror led to him earning the nickname 'Bitter' Bierce.

GROUCHO MARX

And finally, the talented US comedian whose first name suggests grouchiness itself, Groucho Marx (1895–1977). In the legendary films he made with his brothers Chico, Harpo and Zeppo, Groucho's immediately identifiable character was that of a man with a huge cigar, a big moustache, and a sizeable wit to match. After his film career, he continued in entertainment as master of ceremonies of a television series, *You Bet Your Life*, and wrote the autobiographical *Groucho and Me* (1959) and *Memoirs of a Mangy Lover* (1964).

Many of the quotable quotes from this caustic wit are arguably of the humorously grumpy variety:

The Medium is the Massage

'I was married by a judge.
I should have asked for a jury.'

'I worked myself up from nothing
to a state of extreme poverty.'

'No one is completely unhappy
at the failure of his best friend.'

'There is one way to find out if a man
is honest – ask him. If he says "Yes",
you know he is crooked.'

Why, I'd horse-whip you if I had a horse.

You've got the brain of a four-year-old boy,
and I'll bet he was glad to get rid of it.

Now there's a man with an open mind –
you can feel the breeze from here!

Quotable Quibbles
About Entertainment and the Media

A medium, so called because it is neither rare
nor well done.
ERNIE KOVACS, US entertainer
(an attributed remark about television)

*

I got tired of seeing television shows that consist of a car
crash, a gunman, and a hooker talking to a black pimp.
It was cheaper to do a new series than to throw out
my family's television sets.
BILL COSBY, US actor,
author and comedian

*

I read the newspaper avidly.
It is my one form of continuous fiction.
ANEURIN BEVAN, Welsh politician

It is stupidvision – where most of the presenters
look like they have to pretend to be stupid because
they think their audience is . . . It patronizes.
It talks to the vacuum cleaner and the washing machine
without much contact with the human brain.
Polly Toynbee, British journalist
(said of daytime television)

*

The only 'ism' Hollywood believes in is plagiarism.
Dorothy Parker,
US humorist, critic and writer

*

This is not a book that should be tossed lightly aside.
It should be hurled with great force.
Dorothy Parker (referring to a novel
by Benito Mussolini)

*

She ran the whole gamut of the emotions from A to B.
Dorothy Parker (referring to
Katharine Hepburn on Broadway; attributed)

*

'Media' is a word that has come to mean bad journalism.
Graham Greene, British novelist

*

Television? The word is half Greek and half Latin.
No good can come of it.
C. P. Scott, British journalist (attributed)

Are You a Miserable Old Git?

TV is faster-paced generally these days – soaps are mainly responsible for that. The attention span has dropped so that few scenes these days last longer than two minutes. I sound like a grumpy old man. Hell, I am!
GARY RUSSELL, British writer and producer

*

Chewing gum for the eyes.
FRANK LLOYD WRIGHT, US architect
(an attributed remark made about television)

*

I've finally figured out why soap operas are, and logically should be, so popular with generations of housebound women. They are the only place in our culture where grown-up men take seriously all the things that grown-up women have to deal with all day long.
GLORIA STEINEM, US feminist and writer

*

Lloyd Webber's music is everywhere, but so is AIDS.
SIR MALCOLM WILLIAMSON,
Master of the Queen's Music
(said of Andrew Lloyd Webber's musical
Sunset Boulevard)

*

An American musical so bad that at times I longed for the boy-meets-tractor theme of Soviet drama.
BERNARD LEVIN, British journalist
(said of the eminently forgettable 1961 Rodgers and Hammerstein musical *Flower Drum Song*)

In old days men had the rack. Now they have the press.
Oscar Wilde, Irish playwright and poet

*

A magazine is simply a device
to induce people to read advertising.
James Collins, US advertising executive

*

Advertising – a judicious mixture of flattery and threats.
Northrop Frye, Canadian literary critic

*

In the United States today, we have more than our share
of the nattering nabobs of negativism. They have
formed their own 4-H Club – the 'hopeless,
hysterical hypochondriacs of history'.
Spiro T. Agnew, US Vice-President
(said of the press in 1970)

[59]

A reporter is a man who has renounced everything in life
but the world, the flesh, and the devil.
David Murray, British journalist and writer

✳

A great many people now reading and writing
would be better employed keeping rabbits.
Edith Sitwell, British author

Abstract art? A product of the untalented
sold by the unprincipled to the utterly bewildered.
Al Capp, US cartoonist

✳

An editor should have a pimp for a brother
so he'd have someone to look up to.
Gene Fowler, US journalist

✳

I don't hate the press: I find a lot of it very unpalatable.
But if that's the way they want to behave . . .
Prince Philip, Duke of Edinburgh

I'm sure they have a special screening where they go,
'I'm sorry but you don't appear to be a nutter, so we can't
actually put you on the air.' Any debate about war or
dictators will go straight to Hitler. Or any debate about
technology will go straight to 'Well, we've put a man
on the moon.' There's actually a rule in the BBC Charter
which says that only people talking in total clichés
are allowed to be put in these programmes.
John O'Farrell, British writer

*

Editor: a person employed by a newspaper
whose business it is to separate the wheat from
the chaff and to see that chaff is printed.
Elbert Hubbard,
US writer, printer and editor

*

Television was the ultimate evidence of cultural anaemia.
Roy A. K. Heath,
Guyanese novelist and teacher

*

The fact that a man is a newspaper reporter
is evidence of some flaw of character.
Lyndon B. Johnson, US President

*

It used to be that we in films were the lowest form of art.
Now we have something to look down on.
Billy Wilder, Austrian-born US film director,
writer and producer (said of television)

Are You a Miserable Old Git?

From any cross-section of ads, the general advertiser's attitude would seem to be: if you are a lousy, smelly, idle, underprivileged and oversexed status-seeking neurotic moron, give me your money.
Kenneth Bromfield,
British advertising artist

*

When distant and unfamiliar and complex things are communicated to great masses of people, the truth suffers a considerable and often a radical distortion. The complex is made over into the simple, the hypothetical into the dogmatic, and the relative into an absolute.
Walter Lippmann, US writer and journalist

*

The celebrity is a person
who is known for his well-knownness.
Daniel J. Boorstin, US writer and historian

*

Perfume ads may not tell you anything about the products they're selling, but they do accurately describe the state of your mind if you drink some.
David Quantick, British comedian and writer

*

The near-equivalent of actual conmen, loan-ad presenters are inches away from being criminals. They are saying, 'I am famous so take my advice and get more into debt than you were before.' Vile filth.
David Quantick

An author is a fool who, not content with having bored those who have lived with him, insists on boring future generations.
Charles, Baron de Montesquieu,
French philosopher, writer and lawyer

*

Hollywood is a place where they'll pay you a thousand dollars for a kiss and fifty cents for your soul.
Marilyn Monroe, US film actress

A character actor is one who cannot act and therefore makes an elaborate study of disguise and stage tricks by which acting can be grotesquely simulated.
George Bernard Shaw,
Irish dramatist and writer (attributed)

*

Acting is the most minor of gifts. After all, Shirley Temple could do it when she was four.
Katharine Hepburn,
US film actress (attributed)

[63]

Acting is therefore the lowest of the arts,
if it is an art at all.
GEORGE MOORE, Irish writer

∗

Actors should be treated like cattle.
ALFRED HITCHCOCK, British-born US film director

∗

The media. It sounds like a convention of spiritualists.
TOM STOPPARD, playwright and screenwriter

∗

All Stanislavsky ever said was, 'Avoid generalities.'
ANTHONY HOPKINS, British actor

∗

No! Not at any price . . . When I am through with this
picture I hope never to hear of Dracula again. I cannot
stand it . . . I do not intend that it shall possess me.
No one knows what I suffer from the role.
BÉLA LUGOSI, Hungarian-born US film actor
(he'd been asked to play the role on stage,
and got rather grumpy about it)

Oh, my God! Remember you're in Egypt.
The *skay* is only seen in Kensington.
HERBERT BEERBOHM TREE, British actor and
theatrical impresario (an actress had taken her affected
pronunciation of 'sky' to Egypt with her; attributed)

*

Well, I suppose the media are such a major industry now,
and it needs feeding, so rather than wait for celebrity to
happen they sort of invent it in order to report on it.
Do you know what I mean? You don't necessarily have
to wait any more. You just make it up as you go along.
BILL NIGHY, British actor

*

Seventeen years of reputation doesn't really matter
to a media that sniffs blood.
ANITA RODDICK, British business executive
and Body Shop founder (said of a fall
in the Body Shop's fortunes)

*

Advertising may be described as the science of arresting
human intelligence long enough to get money from it.
STEPHEN LEACOCK,
Canadian humorist and economist

*

She looked as though butter wouldn't melt
in her mouth – or anywhere else.
ELSA LANCHESTER, British-born US actress
(referring to Maureen O'Hara; attributed)

[65]

Advertising . . . legitimizes the idealized, stereotyped roles of women as temptress, wife, mother, and sex object.
Lucy Komisar, US writer

∗

Don't Tell My Mother I Work in an Advertising Agency –
She Thinks I Play Piano in a Whorehouse
Jacques Séguéla, US advertising executive
(title of a memoir about being an advertising executive)

∗

I think that I shall never see
A billboard lovely as a tree.
Perhaps unless the billboards fall,
I'll never see a tree at all.
Ogden Nash,
US poet and humorist

∗

I put on the news and discovered that they took Trevor McDonald's desk away. He's just standing there, and you think, 'What's that all about?' And gradually it dawns on you that somebody must have said, 'I've got an idea that will really make the news-viewing experience much improved – we'll take your desk away.' How do they possibly see this sort of thing as an improvement?
Bill Bryson, US writer

∗

Some of the greatest love affairs I've known involved one actor – unassisted.
Wilson Mizner, US playwright (attributed)

History will see advertising as one of the real evil things
of our time. It is stimulating people constantly
to want things, want this, want that.
Malcolm Muggeridge,
British journalist and commentator (attributed)

*

I have had my aerials removed –
it's the moral equivalent of a prostate operation.
Malcolm Muggeridge

*

I don't care for modern films.
Cars crashing over cliffs
and close-ups of people's feet.
Lillian Gish, US actress

*

The gift of broadcasting is, without question, the lowest
human capacity to which any man could attain.
Harold Nicolson,
British diplomat, writer and critic

Rock journalism is people who can't write interviewing
people who can't talk for people who can't read.
FRANK ZAPPA, US composer
and rock musician

＊

Any little pinhead who makes one picture is called a 'star'.
HUMPHREY BOGART, US actor (attributed)

＊

I didn't like the play, but then I saw it under adverse
conditions – the curtain was up.
GROUCHO MARX, US comedian

＊

Educational television should be absolutely forbidden.
It can only lead to unreasonable disappointment
when your child discovers that the letters of the alphabet
do not leap up out of books and dance around
with royal-blue chickens.
FRAN LEBOWITZ, US journalist

＊

You can fool all of the people all of the time if the
advertising is right and the budget is big enough.
JOSEPH E. LEVINE, US film producer

＊

When a man throws an empty cigarette package from an
automobile, he is liable to a fine of fifty dollars. When a
man throws a billboard across a view, he is richly rewarded.
PAT BROWN, US politician

If there's anything disgusting about the movie business,
it's the whoredom of my peers.
Sean Penn,
US actor and film director

*

Jazz: music invented for the torture of imbeciles.
Henry VanDyke,
US clergyman and educator

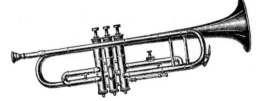

He's the kind of guy that, when he dies,
he gives God a bad time for making him bald.
Marlon Brando, US actor
(referring to Frank Sinatra)

*

An actor's a guy who, if you ain't talking about him,
ain't listening.
Marlon Brando

*

Television is the first truly democratic culture – the first
culture available to everybody and entirely governed
by what the people want. The most terrifying thing
is what the people do want.
Clive Barnes, British drama critic

I hate television. I hate it as much as peanuts.
But I can't stop eating peanuts.
Orson Welles, US actor, director,
producer and writer

*

I would just like to mention Robert Houdini,
who in the eighteenth century invented the
vanishing-birdcage trick and the theatre matinée –
may he rot and perish. Good afternoon.
Orson Welles
(addressing the audience
at the end of a matinée performance)

*

Everyone denies I am a genius –
but nobody ever called me one!
Orson Welles (attributed)

It is all very well to be able to write books,
but can you waggle your ears?
J. M. Barrie, Scottish dramatist
and novelist (said to H. G. Wells)

Bogart's a helluva nice guy till 11.30 p.m.
After that he thinks he's Bogart.
Dave Chausen, US restaurateur

*

As a kisser, Bogart set an awful example.
His mouth addressed a woman's lips with the quivering
nibble of a horse closing in on an apple.
Lance Morrow, US journalist

Directing her was like directing Lassie.
You needed fourteen takes to get each one of them right.
Otto Preminger,
Austrian-born US film director and producer
(referring to directing Marilyn Monroe; attributed)

*

A flock of beetle-brained windsuckers with necks hinged
so they can say yes to Darryl Zanuck.
S. J. Perelman, US humorist
(said of the Hollywood set)

Television is an invention that permits you
to be entertained in your living room by people
you wouldn't have in your home.
DAVID FROST, British TV personality

*

All the personality of a paper cup.
RAYMOND CHANDLER,
US writer (said of Hollywood)

*

The media, far from being a conspiracy to dull
the political sense of the people, could be viewed
as a conspiracy to disguise the extent
of political indifference.
DAVID RIESMAN, US sociologist

*

Hanging is too good for a man who makes puns:
he should be drawn and quoted.
FRED ALLEN, US comedian

*

Imitation is the sincerest form of television.
FRED ALLEN

*

Ten million dollars' worth of intricate
and ingenious machinery functioning elaborately
to put skin on baloney.
GEORGE JEAN NATHAN, US critic,
author and editor (said of Hollywood)

For an actress to be a success she must have the face of
Venus, the brains of Minerva, the grace of Terpsichore,
the memory of Macaulay, the figure of Juno, and the hide
of a rhinoceros.
ETHEL BARRYMORE, US actress

There is one thing on earth more terrible
than English music, and that is English painting.
HEINRICH HEINE, German poet

*

A critic is a bundle of biases held loosely together
by a sense of taste.
WHITNEY BALLIETT, US writer

*

If they can take it for ten minutes, then play it for fifteen.
That's our policy. Always leave them wanting less.
ANDY WARHOL, US artist and filmmaker

*

People will cross the road at the risk of losing their own
lives in order to say, 'We saw you on the telly.'
QUENTIN CRISP, British writer, actor and raconteur

TV . . . is our latest medium –
we call it a medium because nothing's well done.
Goodman Ace,
US radio and TV writer and comedian

*

It's very hard for an actor to open his gob without
whatever he says sounding risible. If you even whisper
a murmur of complaint, you're labelled a po-faced git
who can't see the funny side of things.
Kenneth Branagh,
British actor and film director (attributed)

*

Theatre director: a person engaged by the management
to conceal the fact that the players cannot act.
James Agate, British film
and drama critic (attributed)

*

Movies are an inherently stupid art form that often relies
on scams, tricks, stunts, gambits, ploys, ruses or gags that
are logically or physically impossible, and often both.
Joe Queenan, US journalist and writer

*

Between 1956 and 1969, Elvis Presley, in his spare time
from being the biggest rock'n'roll star of all time,
managed to make thirty-one of the worst movies in
motion-picture history.
Joe Queenan

A good storyteller is a person who has a good memory
and hopes other people haven't.
Irvine S. Cobb, US humorist
and journalist (attributed)

O! it offends me to the soul to hear a robustious
periwig-pated fellow tear a passion to tatters, to very rags,
to split the ears of the groundlings, who for the most part
are capable of nothing but inexplicable dumb-shows and
noise: I would have such a fellow whipped for o'erdoing
Termagant; it out-herods Herod: pray you, avoid it.
William Shakespeare,
from *Hamlet*, Act III, Scene II
(Hamlet is grumpily instructing his players)

*

I'm always amazed that people will actually choose to sit
in front of the television and just be savaged by stuff that
belittles their intelligence.
Alice Walker,
US novelist and poet

[75]

The words, 'Kiss Kiss Bang Bang', which I saw on an Italian movie poster, are perhaps the briefest statement imaginable of the basic appeal of movies.
PAULINE KAEL, US film critic

*

Hollywood will rot on the windmills of Eternity
Hollywood whose movies stick in the throat of God
Yes Hollywood will get what it deserves.
ALLEN GINSBERG, US poet

*

It's just like having a licence to print your own money.
LORD THOMSON OF FLEET,
Canadian-born British newspaper proprietor
(talking about television)

*

Why should people go out and pay money
to see bad movies when they can stay at home
and see bad television for nothing?
SAMUEL GOLDWYN,
Polish-born US film producer

*

His ears make him look like a taxicab
with both doors open.
HOWARD HUGHES,
US film producer and business executive
(talking of Clark Gable; attributed)

The Merits of Being a Grumpy Old Pessimist, or Why it makes sense to think the worst will always happen

'Always borrow money from a pessimist –
he doesn't expect to be paid back.'
ANONYMOUS

By their very nature, most miserable old gits have a propensity for pessimism – indeed, they wouldn't know what to do with themselves if they didn't have the freedom to emit a regular flow of gloomy whinges across an endless range of subjects. Sample gripes (which should be delivered in suitably lugubrious tones) include:

'I'd better take my umbrella with me because I'm bound to get soaked if I leave the house without one . . . even though rain hasn't been forecast.'

'I was standing in that queue for five minutes until someone looked up and noticed me – I may as well be invisible.'

'There's absolutely no point in my applying for that job because I probably won't even get an interview.'

'I don't know why I even have a phone because nobody ever bothers to call me.'

'Why should I bother buying a Lottery ticket every week? I'm never going to win anything.'

'Why is it always me who has to walk the dog?'

Although it's true to say that such a consistently negative attitude rarely generates much sympathy in others, at least if you expect that the worst is always certain to happen, then it's a bit of a surprise when something actually works out in your favour. Equally, if you expect the worst to happen, and it does, you don't have to bear the disappointment of having your hopes ground mercilessly into the ground. Every cloud, eh?

Quotable Querulous Quibbles About Pessimism

We all agree that pessimism is a mark
of superior intellect.
J. K. GALBRAITH, US economist

*

A pessimist thinks that everybody is as nasty
as himself, and hates them for it.
GEORGE BERNARD SHAW, Irish dramatist and writer

*

The most prolific period of pessimism comes at
twenty-one, or thereabouts, when the first attempt
is made to translate dreams into reality.
HEYWOOD BROUN, US journalist

*

Some people are so fond of ill luck
that they run halfway to meet it.
DOUGLAS JERROLD, British writer

*

The optimist proclaims that we live in the best of all
possible worlds; and the pessimist fears this is true.
JAMES BRANCH CABELL, US author

*

I'm a pessimist because of intelligence,
but an optimist because of will.
ANTONIO GRAMSCI,
Italian Marxist thinker and activist

[79]

The nice part about being a pessimist
is that you are constantly being either proven right
or pleasantly surprised.
GEORGE F. WILL,
US columnist and commentator

*

An optimist laughs to forget.
A pessimist forgets to laugh.
ANONYMOUS

*

Pessimist: one who, when he has the choice
of two evils, chooses both.
OSCAR WILDE,
Irish playwright and poet

*

My pessimism goes to the point of suspecting the
sincerity of the pessimists.
EDMOND ROSTAND, French playwright

*

A pessimist is one who builds dungeons in the air.
WALTER WINCHELL,
US newspaper and radio commentator

*

A pessimist is a man who has been compelled to live
with an optimist.
ELBERT HUBBARD,
US writer, printer and editor

A pessimist sees only the dark side of the clouds,
and mopes; a philosopher sees both sides, and shrugs;
an optimist doesn't see the clouds at all –
he's walking on them.
Leonard Louis Levinson, US writer

✳

An optimist stays up until midnight to see the new year
in. A pessimist stays up to make sure the old year leaves.
Bill Vaughan, US journalist and author

✳

The optimist says, 'My cup runneth over, what a
blessing.' The pessimist says, 'My cup runneth over,
what a mess.'
Anonymous

✳

An optimist is merely an ex-pessimist with his pockets
full of money, his digestion in good condition,
and his wife in the country.
Helen Rowland, US writer

Both optimists and pessimists contribute to our society.
The optimist invents the airplane
and the pessimist the parachute.
GIL STERN, US writer

A pessimist is a man who thinks all women are bad.
An optimist is a man who hopes they are.
CHAUNCEY MITCHELL DEPEW, US politician and wit

*

An optimist is a guy that has never had much experience.
DON MARQUIS, US writer and humorist

*

The place where optimism most flourishes
is the lunatic asylum.
HAVELOCK ELLIS, British sexologist

*

Pessimism, when you get used to it,
is just as agreeable as optimism.
ARNOLD BENNETT, British writer

Rantings of a Miserable Old Git: Part II

This section bemoans political correctness. You never see it described as mere 'political correctness' these days: it's always 'political correctness gone mad'. PCGM, we've called it.

- In 2005, police in London were told they couldn't call people a good egg or a bad egg because it was deemed racist, i.e. it could be confused with Cockney rhyming slang, because 'egg and spoon' rhymes with 'coon'. PCGM or what? These terms have been in circulation since the middle of the nineteenth century, for goodness' sake, and anyway, when did you last hear a British bobby call somebody a good egg? Or even a bad egg? 'I say, old chap, I don't suppose you'd be a good egg and accompany me down to the station, would you? It's just that there's this jolly old suspicion going around, don't you know, that you've been a bit of a bad egg. Now, if you'd just slip into these little bracelets we can jolly well pop off down to the police station and be there in time for cucumber sandwiches, toasted crumpets and a nice pot of tea . . .'

• The BBC programme *Country File* reported in February 2005 that a 'diversity review' by the Countryside Agency cost a million quid of the nation's money and its job was to find out why some people don't visit the countryside. The conclusion was that some designated walks were seen as too white and too middle-class. Isn't it obvious that it's going to be people who live in or near the countryside who mainly walk *in* the countryside, and those from ethnic minorities whom they'd like to encourage live mainly in cities and, like many city-dwellers, can't just nip out into the country for a stroll when they feel like it.

• More PCGM, this time from the Metropolitan Police. In 2004 they decided to insult black people by declaring that they would in future be called 'visible minority ethnics' instead of the previous 'black minority ethnic' and 'black ethnic minority'. Goodness knows how much money it cost to get all the memos out for an amendment that doesn't alter things very much. In response to this PCGM, a sensible sort of chap wrote to *The Daily Telegraph* in December 2004 saying that, if an old lady were to be mugged by a black man with a limp who spoke with a Welsh accent, 'they will now ask the public to help them find "a mobility-challenged visible minority ethnic person speaking with a distinct invisible minority ethnic accent".' Another man wrote that, when he visited Nigeria, local people, and in particular the children, called him *'onyeocha'* or *'oyibo'*, which translate as 'white man'. 'Do I take

[84]

offence?' he asked. 'No, I love it because it's always said with a smile and there's an honesty in saying things as you see them. Would I like to be called a "visible minority ethnic"? No, that's offensive.' Well, that's putting it in black and white.

• Teachers at a primary school in Smethwick in the West Midlands were told in 2003 to stop using red ink when marking their pupils' work because of its 'negative connotations'; they were advised to use green ink instead. Perhaps the change in policy arose from a concern that their young charges might somehow be scarred for life through being subjected to the horrors of the dreaded red pen. Get used to it, kids – life's a bitch and then you die . . .

• A programme on Century FM in the north-east of England in 2004 had people ringing in saying that kids at school were being told to sing 'Baa, baa, green sheep', and a man working for a transport firm had been told he couldn't use the term 'dipstick', but had to say 'oil-level indicator'.

- Councils have taken to banning the word 'Christmas' from displays and lights because of some PCGM idea that it might offend people of other religions (or none). Have they gone stark raving mad? Have we reached a point where we can no longer accept the beliefs of others if they happen to be different from our own? To Christians, Christmas is the second of two significant annual celebrations, while to non-believers it merely heralds a time of celebration, holiday and merry-making. Let's leave it at that, shall we, and avoid causing worse offence to Christians by attempting to deny its very existence.

- In autumn 2004 some British schools banned the time-honoured game of conkers, because they thought it might be dangerous. No conkers? That's bonkers! Some school authorities even went so far as to say there was a danger of nut allergy. *What?* Conkers aren't nuts, but clearly these officials and head teachers are . . .

Out of the Mouths of Babes, or Why children should be fried, casseroled or both

'Two things should be cut: the second act
and the child's throat.'
NOËL COWARD, British playwright and actor
(referring to a child actor)

Let's get one thing straight right from the start. We are not talking only about *your* children in this section, dear reader, even though your own may be naughty little tykes at times. No, we are talking chiefly about *other people's* children (although you may recognize yours here somewhere), as it's mostly other people's children who get you grumpy and tend to bring out the miserable old git in you.

For a start, there are too many of them. Children in general, that is, not just the little devils who pull your flowers up and speak obscenities into their mobile phones when they're standing right next to you. In bygone days, it made sense to produce lots of the little devils in order to survive, but not any more.

When very young they have a propensity for making noises, smells and messes at both ends, making you wish you could take out an antisocial-behaviour order on them. Children are mad. They need to see a shrink. They need to be put out of *our* misery. Then they begin to cultivate zits, creating fascinating facial patterns in which you can make out Ursa Minor, the Pleiades and the Plough, and they insist on dressing in loose, baggy, unattractive clothes no normal person would be seen dead in. And when they reach their teens they start to roam shopping malls in hoodies and huge trainers, frightening old ladies who think they're marauding hobbits.

And why can't they talk properly? They go around saying 'innit?' and 'well wicked' and 'cool', 'like' and 'right?' Or they just grunt and look morose. If you're an adult – especially a parent – as far as they're concerned you might as well be from another planet. You've fed them, clothed them, had your house trashed by them, and they loathe you for it.

Doesn't it make you grumpy when ...

. . . you go out with friends for a meal at a local pub or restaurant, and the table next to yours becomes occupied by a family with a minimum of two screaming kids in tow? Not only can you no longer hear yourselves over the escalating din at the adjoining table, but there's almost nothing you can do to resolve the situation: if you complain, you'll simply become the baddie of the piece. Better to wait until one child stabs its sibling with a fork, thus necessitating a hasty hospital visit . . . or is that just wishful thinking?

These days, of course, kids aren't happy unless they've got a gadget – and it's usually something noisy that will be out of fashion in about six minutes, when they'll demand (without grace) and usually receive (without gratitude) the next upgrade, whether it be a mobile phone, iPod or computer.

Not only can kids be annoying, but their parents have a tendency to get up one's nose as well, especially at certain times of the day. Take, for example, the school run: it's easy to forget about it until you find yourself caught up in a sea of SUVs, sporty BMWs, and oversized people-carriers (usually containing a single small child), all hogging the roads in an effort to pick up or drop off their little dears in the most aggressive manner possible. What hope have the kids got with parents like that?

It would seem we're not alone in expressing one or two mild reservations about kids. There are a number of others who find these spawn of the Devil less than endearing, too . . .

Quotable Querulous Quibbles About Kids

I love children – especially when they cry,
for then someone takes them away.
NANCY MITFORD, British writer (attributed)

Are You a Miserable Old Git?

The young always have the same problem – how to rebel
and conform at the same time. They have now solved
this by defying their parents and copying one another.
QUENTIN CRISP, British writer,
actor and raconteur

*

Children aren't happy with nothing to ignore,
And that's what parents were created for.
OGDEN NASH, US poet and humorist

*

I love all my children, but some of them I don't like.
LILLIAN CARTER, US nurse
and mother of President Jimmy Carter

*

Sometimes when I look at my children I say to myself,
'Lillian, you should have stayed a virgin.'
LILLIAN CARTER

*

Children and babies should be where they belong –
at home, in nurseries, in casseroles.
JIM DUCKER, British writer (said of kids in pubs)

*

When childhood dies, its corpses are called adults and
they enter society, one of the politer names of hell.
That is why we dread children, even if we love them.
They show us the state of our decay.
BRIAN ALDISS, British science-fiction writer

I like children – fried.
W. C. Fields, US actor and comedian

∗

It is . . . sometimes easier to head an institute for the
study of child guidance than it is to turn one brat into a
decent human being.
Joseph Wood Krutch, US essayist and naturalist

∗

It was no wonder that people were so horrible when they
started life as children.
Kingsley Amis, British novelist

∗

Schoolchildren are like normal children only psychotic.
They are armed, dangerous, violent, rude, unkempt and
obsessed with smoking behind the bike sheds.
David Quantick, British comedian and writer

∗

The nice thing about having relatives' kids around
is that they go home.
Cliff Richard, British pop singer

People treat children as though there's something wrong
with them because they're ignorant and small. They say,
'I'm so worried about Alexander's development. I mean,
he's got no grasp of bonded numbers, no concept
of phonics, his hand-to-eye coordination is all over
the place. I mean, goodness knows what he's going
to be like when he's born.'
JEREMY HARDY, British comedian

∗

My theory is, children should be born
without parents – if born they must be.
LANGSTON HUGHES, US novelist,
playwright and short-story writer

∗

Never have children, only grandchildren.
GORE VIDAL, US novelist

∗

The real menace in dealing with a five-year-old is that in
no time at all you begin to sound like a five-year-old.
JEAN KERR, US playwright and humorist

∗

There was a little girl
Who had a little curl
Right in the middle of her forehead;
When she was good
She was very very good,
But when she was bad she was horrid.
HENRY WADSWORTH LONGFELLOW, US poet

The thing that best defines a child is the total inability
to receive information from anything not plugged in.
BILL COSBY, US actor, author and comedian

*

There is no more sombre enemy of good art
than the pram in the hall.
CYRIL CONNOLLY, British writer and journalist

*

They never lynch children, babies, no matter
what they do they are whitewashed in advance.
SAMUEL BECKETT, Irish dramatist, novelist and poet
(from *The Expelled and Other Novellas*)

*

All God's children are not beautiful.
Most of God's children are, in fact, barely presentable.
FRAN LEBOWITZ, US journalist

Fooling All of the People, or Why politicians are held in such contempt

'If presidents don't do it to their wives,
they do it to the country.'
MEL BROOKS, US film director

How do you know when politicians are lying? Simple – their lips are moving. In fact the only time you can be sure that politicians are telling the truth is when they're calling each other 'liar'. To most people they're just a bunch of slimy, devious, scheming, underhand, conniving, self-seeking, cheating, fraudulent crooks.

What's most annoying is that there isn't a constant or regular appraisal that keeps them on their toes in their cosy little ivory towers, either. In industry, you make money for your bosses or you're out, but in politics, provided you can keep pulling the wool over the eyes of your constituents and ask enough questions in Parliament to be seen to be doing something, you're safe. The weak are a long time in politics.

Did you hear the one about the chap who went for a brain transplant? The surgeon says, 'We've got the brain of a polymath – a man who was well versed in the sciences, the arts, the humanities, and he was a Nobel winner to boot. That'll cost you fifty grand. Then there's this one from a politician. That'll knock you back a hundred grand.' When the chap asks why the politician's brain is twice as expensive, the surgeon replies, 'Because it's never been used.'

They can be a grumpy old lot as well. Current Chancellor of the Exchequer Gordon Brown, Britain's Prime Minister-in-waiting, has turned grumpiness into a fine art. Although those who know him say he has a sense of humour, perhaps he should think about showing it during the Budget, by telling a few jokes before embarking on the tedium of reading out all the figures.

The nation's greatest statesman, Winston Churchill, was renowned for his bouts of grumpiness, but with the added bonus that he could also be a witty grouch: when he found himself seated next to the Director General of the BBC, Lord Reith, a tall Presbyterian Scot of gloomy aspect, Churchill was heard to mutter, 'Who will rescue me from this Wuthering Height?'

Then there was that grump of all grumps, the late Edward Heath, who went on a sulk that lasted about thirty years after the Iron Lady nudged him out of the Tory leader's job in 1975. The only really enjoyable (albeit often for the wrong reasons) grouch in the British Cabinet at the time of writing is the Deputy Prime Minister, John Prescott. Apart from hitting people – as he did during the 2001 election campaign (some might say

> ### *Doesn't it make you grumpy when …*
>
> … a politician is faced with an awkward question,
> but on no account will he or she give the interviewer
> a straight answer? No matter how many times the
> same question is asked, the sly politician will give a
> masterclass in evasion and avoidance, ducking and
> diving until the interviewer tires and decides to ask
> another question … which is also shamelessly
> sidestepped, for that is the politician's way.

quite rightly) when some joker threw an egg at him – he has
a face like that of a cross between a bull mastiff and a boxer
dog who's just been hosed down after pissing on the offside
wheel of a Jag (or two Jags). He has jowls and dewlaps that
must weigh at least a stone, and is renowned for mangling
his syntax in such a way that it makes the ramblings of a
five-year-old on an Internet bulletin board read like the
views of an Oxford grammar professor.

As a politician, Prescott could never be called smarmy,
but a great many others can, and don't they get right up
your nose? They're oleaginous in their propensity for
glutinously sticking to the party line, no matter how
totally wrong it is – so greasily sycophantic you could fry
chips on them.

Politicians? You can keep 'em. Whatever the party. We
make no excuses for ranting about the lot that are currently
in power, but they're all just as bad, and if one of the other
parties were in power we'd probably be saying much the
same. But enough of our futile whingeing – let's look at
what others have had to say about this loathsome species …

Quotable Querulous Quibbles About Politics

The trouble with this country is that there are too many
politicians who believe, with a conviction based on
experience, that you can fool all of the people
all of the time.
Franklin P. Adams, US journalist and radio
personality (an allusion to Lincoln's oft-quoted
'You may fool all the people some of the time;
you can even fool some of the people all the time;
but you can't fool all the people all the time')

Politicians are like nappies:
they should be changed often –
and for the same reason.
Barry Cryer, British comedian

*

When the politicians complain that TV turns
their proceedings into a circus, it should be made plain
that the circus was already there, and that TV has merely
demonstrated that not all the performers are well trained.
Ed Murrow, US journalist (attributed)

Are You a Miserable Old Git?

Any man who is under thirty, and is not a liberal,
has no heart; and any man who is over thirty,
and is not a conservative, has no brains.
Winston Churchill, British Prime Minister

*

A sheep in sheep's clothing.
Winston Churchill
(said of Labour Prime Minister Clement Attlee)

*

Political skill . . . the ability to foretell what is going
to happen tomorrow, next week, next month
and next year. And to have the ability afterwards
to explain why it didn't happen.
Winston Churchill

*

In war you can only be killed once,
but in politics – many times.
Winston Churchill (attributed)

Fooling All of the People

Politics is not the art of the possible. It consists in choosing between the disastrous and the unpalatable.
JOHN KENNETH GALBRAITH,
Canadian-born US economist
('Politics is the art of the possible' is attributed
to the nineteenth-century German Chancellor,
Prince Otto von Bismarck)

*

Nothing is so admirable in politics
as a short memory.
JOHN KENNETH GALBRAITH

*

There are times in politics when you must be
on the right side and lose.
JOHN KENNETH GALBRAITH

*

Democracy consists of choosing your dictators,
after they've told you what you think it is
you want to hear.
ALAN COREN, British humorist

*

There is one rule for politicians all over the world:
don't say in power what you say in opposition;
if you do, you only have to carry out what the
other fellows have found impossible.
JOHN GALSWORTHY,
British novelist and playwright

A group of politicians deciding to dump a President
because his morals are bad is like the Mafia getting
together to bump off the Godfather for not going
to church on Sunday.
Russell Baker, US humorist

*

Alliance, *n.*: in international politics, the union of two
thieves who have their hands so deeply inserted into each
other's pocket that they cannot safely plunder a third.

Battle, *n.*: a method of untying with the teeth a political
knot that will not yield to the tongue.

Conservative, *n.*: a statesman who is enamoured of
existing evils, as distinguished from the Liberal who
wishes to replace them with others.

History, *n.*: an account, mostly false, of events, mostly
unimportant, which are brought about by rulers, mostly
knaves, and soldiers, mostly fools.

Opposition, *n.*: in politics the party that prevents the
government from running amuck by hamstringing it.

Politics, *n.*: A strife of interests masquerading as a contest
of principles.

Referendum, *n.*: A law for submission of proposed
legislation to a popular vote to learn the nonsensus of
public opinion.

Ambrose Bierce,
US writer and journalist

[100]

Politics are for foreigners with their endless wrongs and paltry rights. Politics are a lousy way to get things done. Politics are, like God's infinite mercy, a last resort.
P. J. O'ROURKE,
US satirist and journalist

*

Hell, I never vote *for* anybody. I always vote *against*.
W. C. FIELDS, US actor and comedian

Why should I question the monkey,
when I can question the organ grinder?
ANEURIN BEVAN, Welsh politician
(preferring to question Prime Minister Churchill
rather than the Foreign Secretary)

*

And you call that statesmanship.
I call it an emotional spasm.
ANEURIN BEVAN,
(speaking at a Labour Party conference)

What do you want to be a sailor for? There are greater
storms in politics than you will ever find at sea.
Piracy, broadsides, blood on the decks.
You will find them all in politics.
David Lloyd George,
British Prime Minister

✳

I have come to the conclusion that politics is too serious
a matter to be left to the politicians.
Charles de Gaulle,
French President, soldier and statesman

✳

Since a politician never believes what he says, he is
surprised when others believe him.
Charles de Gaulle

✳

It's a great country, where anybody can grow up to be
president – except me.
Barry Goldwater, US politician

✳

Vic Oliver (Churchill's son-in-law): Who, in your
opinion, is the greatest statesman you know?
Churchill (smartly): Benito Mussolini.
Oliver: *What?* Why?
Churchill: Mussolini is the only statesman who had
the requisite courage to have his son-in-law executed.
(Sarah Churchill's marriage to the much older
US-Austrian comedian did not last long.)

Politics is perhaps the only profession for which
no preparation is thought necessary.
ROBERT LOUIS STEVENSON,
Scottish novelist, essayist and poet

*

A Conservative government is an organized hypocrisy.
BENJAMIN DISRAELI,
British Prime Minister and writer

A week is a long time in politics.
HAROLD WILSON, British Prime Minister

*

I hate politics and the belief in politics, because it makes
men arrogant, doctrinaire, obstinate, and inhuman.
THOMAS MANN, German writer

*

In politics, what begins in fear usually ends in folly.
SAMUEL TAYLOR COLERIDGE, British poet,
critic and philosopher

The first thing that one loses in politics is one's freedom.
JOAQUIM MARÍA MACHADO DE ASSIS,
Brazilian novelist and short-story writer.

*

Politics is opposed to morality, as philosophy to naïvety.
EMMANUEL LEVINAS,
Lithuanian-born French philosopher

*

Any American who is prepared to run for president
should automatically, by definition, be disqualified
from ever doing so.
GORE VIDAL, US novelist and essayist (attributed)

*

All political lives, unless they are cut off in mid-stream at
a happy juncture, end in failure, because that is the nature
of politics and of human affairs.
ENOCH POWELL, British politician

*

The difference between a Democracy and a Dictatorship
is that in a Democracy you vote first and take orders later;
in a Dictatorship you don't have to waste your time voting.
CHARLES BUKOWSKI, US poet and author

*

He knows nothing and thinks he knows everything.
That points clearly to a political career.
GEORGE BERNARD SHAW,
Irish dramatist and writer

Fooling All of the People

Christchurch was the place where the difference
between the Tories and the Alfred Chicken Party
was that members of the Alfred Chicken Party
ran around with their heads still on.
PHILIP GOLDENBERG, British politician,
referring to a by-election the Tories unexpectedly lost

*

As usual, the Liberals offer a mixture of sound and
original ideas. Unfortunately none of the sound ideas
is original and none of the original ideas is sound.
HAROLD MACMILLAN, British Prime Minister

*

People never lie so much as after a hunt,
during a war or before an election.
PRINCE OTTO VON BISMARCK,
German statesman

Politics are usually the executive expression
of human immaturity.
Vera Brittain, British pacifist and writer

*

Anyone who wants the presidency so much
that he'll spend two years organizing and campaigning
for it is not to be trusted with the office.
David Broder, US journalist

*

Politics is the art of looking for trouble, finding it,
misdiagnosing it, and then misapplying the wrong
remedies.
Groucho Marx, US comedian

*

I have always said, the first Whig was the Devil.
Samuel Johnson, British lexicographer,
critic and essayist

*

I fear my Socialism is purely cerebral; I do not like the
masses in the flesh.
Harold Nicolson, British diplomat,
writer and critic

*

Under democracy one party always devotes its energies to
trying to prove that the other party is unfit to rule – and
both commonly succeed and are right.
H. L. Mencken, US journalist, critic and editor

Rantings of a Miserable Old Git: Part III

SHOPPING – Why does it always seem to be that after queuing in a supermarket for what seems like a week (but is probably about ten minutes), just as you finally reach the front of the queue, another till opens up just next door? You're never that lucky when it comes to choosing queues – you try to go for the shortest, in the hope that it'll be the fastest, but it always ends up taking twice as long as all the others. It's as though whichever queue you stand in, you'll be certain to jinx it.

MOVIE MISERY – Picture the scene: you're in a cinema, the film is just about to start and you've got a clear sight of the screen . . . until some 6-foot-10-inch giant chooses to sit directly in front of you, thus ruining the evening's entertainment. Another surefire way to be antagonized at the movies is to find yourself sitting in close proximity to a serial sweet-muncher who likes nothing more than to extract mint humbugs from deafeningly loud wrappers, slowly, painfully, irritatingly. Even people's popcorn-guzzling antics can be an excruciating distraction.

Transport blues – Why is it that, whenever you arrive early at the railway station, the train you need to catch is delayed for several minutes, forcing you to wait in the cold until it turns up; however, on the days when you get to the station just seconds after the train was due to depart, inevitably it has left on time, the doors closing mockingly as you hurl yourself onto the platform in desperation. What is that all about?

Mobile madness – There are few things worse than having to endure listening to tediously banal mobile-phone conversations while you're travelling home after a hard day at work, particularly when all you want to do is sleep or be left in peace to read a book. These people who feel the need to share the tiresome details of their sad little lives (at full volume) with a carriage full of complete strangers are ignorant, arrogant or just plain selfish. Oh to have the courage to swipe the offending phone from the offensive passenger's hand and lob it through an open window on to the opposite track . . . One day, perhaps.

Tractor tedium – How annoying is it to be motoring casually along scenic country lanes only to end up stuck behind a rambling, manure-carrying tractor, which shows no immediate sign of exiting the winding 'main' road? Invariably the route is littered with blind corners and

dangerous bends, rendering a speedy overtake completely out of the question. No, instead you have to take a deep breath, drop a couple of gears and fall in behind the hulking heap of metal until, after a two-mile crawl, it stops splattering your windscreen with fragments of its stinking load and leaves the road for good.

Quotable Insights on Misery

Most people spend the greater part of their lives making others miserable.
JEAN DE LA BRUYÈRE, French writer

*

We become moral once we are miserable.
MARCEL PROUST, French novelist and critic

*

The secret of being miserable is to have leisure to bother about whether you are happy or not. The cure for it is occupation.
GEORGE BERNARD SHAW, Irish dramatist and writer

*

Most people would rather be certain they're miserable, than risk being happy.
DR ROBERT ANTHONY, US self-help author

Friends *love* misery, in fact. Sometimes, especially if we
are too lucky or too successful or too pretty, our misery
is the only thing that endears us to our friends.
ERICA JONG, US novelist and poet

✳

The minute you leave your house in the morning
you see something that makes you grumpy.
ARTHUR SMITH, British writer and comedian

✳

What fresh hell is this?
DOROTHY PARKER, US humorist, critic and writer
(on the arrival of the morning postal delivery)

The sneeze in English is the harbinger of misery,
even death. I sometimes think the only pleasure
an Englishman has is in passing on his cold germs.
GERALD DURRELL, British naturalist and writer

✳

The misery of a child is interesting to a mother, the
misery of a young man is interesting to a young woman,
the misery of an old man is interesting to nobody.
VICTOR HUGO, French poet, novelist, and playwright

Just because you're miserable doesn't mean
you can't enjoy your life.
ANNETTE GOODHEART, US writer

*

A man's as miserable as he thinks he is.
SENECA, Roman philosopher,
mid-first century CE

*

Those who have had great passions often find
all their lives made miserable in being cured of them.
FRANÇOIS DE LA ROCHEFOUCAULD,
French classical author

*

Money, if it does not bring you happiness,
will at least help you be miserable in comfort.
HELEN GURLEY BROWN,
US editor and writer

Nation Shall Speak Insults Unto Nation, or Foreign bodies and why decent people don't like them

'Hell is a place where the motorists are French, the policemen are German, and the cooks are English.'
Anonymous

Frogs, Krauts, Aussies, Yanks, Poms (usually 'whingeing'), Limeys, Taffies . . . All right, so some people might consider these terms as somewhat offensive, but where's their sense of humour? Let's not get so depressingly politically correct about this. *Vive la différence!* We are what we are – and everyone else is . . . well, foreign.

Not that we think they're inferior, of course. We certainly wouldn't *dream* of saying that. Not even of the French. Well, not much. No, they're just something else. Other. Unfamiliar. Alien. And we know how much they enjoy a laugh at our expense, so why shouldn't we do the same to them?

But Europe? Don't get us started on Europe. The issue is not Europe the continent, but Europe the European Union. Here we are, as diverse a bunch of nations as you can get, and they want to keep making it bigger, still believing that we'll continue to get along like cheery old souls on the glee club annual outing to Cleethorpes. And where does it get us? It gets us edicts that say bananas have to be only of a certain curvature or that cucumbers should be straight, that's where. And how long will it be before the British have to abandon the eminently sensible practice of driving on the left-hand side of the road?

Did you know that, in 2003, trapeze artists and jugglers with the Moscow State Circus were told they would have to wear hard hats during a tour of the UK to comply with EU safety rules? Whether they obeyed the idiotic ruling is not known for certain, but it was introduced nevertheless. Apart from making them look utterly ridiculous, surely the wearing of such bulky headgear could result in more accidents, with performers struggling to maintain a straight face opposite colleagues who look as though they've just stepped off a building site.

> ### Doesn't it make you grumpy when...
>
> ... you've travelled to France with the express intention of improving your knowledge of the French language, and yet whenever you try to make the effort to converse with a local, especially in Paris, your earnest attempts are met with withering disdain and a mockingly condescending reply in English?

Moving on to the Yanks. Oversexed? Not any more, because they're all too fat. Overpaid? You can say that again – you've only got to look at the size of the cars they drive to see that. Over here? Well, treacherously, we Brits are as much over there as the Yanks are over here these days. We should be ashamed of ourselves. After all, culturally, they are the poor relations. The only reason we should be over there is as missionaries. Turn the USA back into a British colony, we say, and show 'em some discipline.

But what an arrogant, loud-mouthed bunch they are, with their gas-guzzling ways, their lack of patience, their zealous Christianity and their teeth. If you can't tell whether a chap's American, count the teeth – all pristine white and neatly lined up like a row of porcelain urinals. And why does every American you see on TV seem to have an analyst? Are they all mad? Well, obviously. Admitting that you're several states short of a Union seems to be part of the American psyche.

Doesn't it make you grumpy when ...

... you go to the US and are confronted by far too much choice, particularly when it comes to ordering food? Nothing is ever straightforward or plain. Burgers come with 101 different extras; it's impossible to order just a simple white coffee; if you ask for chips you get crisps. And the portions? You could feed a British family of four on the contents of one meal alone. It's a wonder the country hasn't sunk under the weight of its hefty occupants.

As for the Aussies – well. They can't make a statement (you know, a straightforward thing with an indicative verb?) or give a command (using the verb imperatively?)

without seeming to ask a question (that is, using an interrogative). You never know whether they're telling you something or asking you something, with that little inflection at the end of *every sodding sentence*.

It's just as well they're at the other side of the world. Although that didn't stop them imposing their vacuous soap operas on us, or the Minogue sisters, or their inferior wine.

But enough of the criticisms about our foreign cousins, for it is also true that many like to turn their back on patriotic feeling in favour of taking a grumpy old sideswipe at their own country and native peoples. We've found a selection of quotable quibbles to prove it.

Quotable Querulous Quibbles About Nationality

The English instinctively admire any man
who has no talent and is modest about it.
JAMES AGATE, British film and drama critic

*

Poor Mexico, so far from God
and so close to the United States.
PORFIRIO DÍAZ, Mexican President,
statesman and soldier

Curse the blasted, jelly-boned swines, the slimy, the
belly-wriggling invertebrates, the miserable sodding
rotters, the flaming sods, the snivelling, dribbling,
dithering, palsied, pulse-less lot that make up England
today. They've got white of egg in their veins, and their
spunk is that watery it's a marvel they can breed.
D. H. Lawrence,
British novelist and poet (in a letter)

✱

In America, only the successful writer is important, in
France all writers are important, in England no writer is
important, and in Australia you have to explain what a
writer is.
Geoffrey Cottrell, British writer

✱

Germans are flummoxed by humour, the Swiss have
no concept of fun, the Spanish think there is nothing
at all ridiculous about eating dinner at midnight,
and the Italians should never, ever have been let in
on the invention of the motor car.
Bill Bryson, US writer

✱

The English think that incompetence
is the same thing as sincerity.
Quentin Crisp, British writer, actor and raconteur

✱

If you're going to America, bring your own food.
Fran Lebowitz, US journalist

The Englishman is never content
but when he is grumbling.
SCOTTISH SAYING

*

Canada could have had French culture, American know-
how, and English government. Instead it got French
government, English know-how and American culture.
JOHN COLOMBO, Canadian writer

*

We know of no spectacle so ridiculous as the British
public in one of its periodical fits of morality.
THOMAS BABINGTON MACAULAY,
British historian and essayist

*

The French are a logical people, which is one reason
the English dislike them so intensely. The other
is that they own France, a country which we have always
judged to be much too good for them.
ROBERT MORLEY, British actor

Are You a Miserable Old Git?

I look upon Switzerland as an inferior sort of Scotland.
SYDNEY SMITH,
British writer and wit

*

Scotland: that garret of the earth, that knuckle-end
of England, that land of Calvin, oatcakes, and sulphur.
SYDNEY SMITH

*

Britain is the only country in the world
where the food is more dangerous than the sex.
JACKIE MASON, US comedian

*

American history is perceived by most people
as a luxury, an entertainment at best, and at worst,
an escape from the present.
CARL N. DEGLER, US historian

Nation Shall Speak Insults Unto Nation

There have been many definitions of hell, but for the
English the best definition is that it is the place where the
Germans are the police, the Swedish are the comedians,
the Italians are the defence force, Frenchmen dig the
roads, the Belgians are the pop singers, the Spanish run
the railways, the Turks cook the food, the Irish are the
waiters, the Greeks run the government, and the
common language is Dutch.
DAVID FROST, British TV presenter,
and ANTHONY JAY, British writer and journalist
(in *To England with Love*)

*

The French are wiser than they seem,
and the Spaniards seem wiser than they are.
FRANCIS BACON, British statesman and philosopher

*

In Russia a man is called reactionary if he objects to
having his property stolen and his wife and children
murdered.
WINSTON CHURCHILL, British Prime Minister

*

Americans always try to do the right thing –
after they've tried everything else.
WINSTON CHURCHILL

*

All the faces here this evening seem to be bloody Poms.
PRINCE CHARLES, heir apparent to the British throne,
said at an Australia Day dinner

The French complain of everything, and always.
NAPOLEON BONAPARTE, French emperor

✱

Basically the French are all peasants.
PABLO PICASSO, Spanish painter

✱

Some people may be Rooshans, and others may be
Prooshans; they are born so, and will please themselves.
Them which is of other natures thinks different.
CHARLES DICKENS, British novelist
(said by Mrs Gamp in *Martin Chuzzlewit*)

✱

Their demeanour is invariably morose, sullen, clownish
and repulsive. I should think there is not, on the face
of the earth, a people so entirely destitute of humour,
vivacity, or the capacity for enjoyment.
CHARLES DICKENS (about Americans)

✱

The 100 per cent American is 99 per cent idiot.
GEORGE BERNARD SHAW, Irish dramatist and writer

Nation Shall Speak Insults Unto Nation

I fear that I have not got much to say about Canada,
not having seen much; what I got by going
to Canada was a cold.
Henry David Thoreau,
US writer, philosopher and naturalist

*

Of course, America had often been discovered
before Columbus, but it had always been hushed up.
Oscar Wilde,
Irish playwright and poet

*

America is one long expectoration.
Oscar Wilde

*

Other people have a nationality.
The Irish and the Jews have a psychosis.
Brendan Behan,
Irish playwright and author

*

The English think soap is civilization.
Heinrich von Treitschke,
German historian and political writer

*

Canada is a country so square
that even the female impersonators are women.
Richard Brenner

English coffee tastes like water
that has been squeezed out of a wet sleeve.
FRED ALLEN, US comedian

*

I know why the sun never sets on the British Empire:
God wouldn't trust an Englishman in the dark.
DUNCAN SPAETH, US university professor

*

Americans are possibly the dumbest people on the
planet . . . We Americans suffer from an enforced
ignorance. We don't know about anything that's
happening outside our country.
Our stupidity is embarrassing.
MICHAEL MOORE, US filmmaker

*

French Canada is a relic of the historical past
preserved by isolation, as Siberian mammoths
are preserved by ice.
GOLDWIN SMITH, British-born
Canadian historian and journalist

Nation Shall Speak Insults Unto Nation

What is not clear is not French; what is not clear is,
moreover, English, Italian, Greek, or Latin.
Antoine de Rivarol, eighteenth-century
French journalist and critic

*

English physicians kill you, the French let you die.
Lord Melbourne, British Prime Minister

*

All Frenchmen want to encroach and extend their
territorial possessions at the expense of other nations.
Their rarity prompts them to be the first nation in the world.
Lord Palmerston, British Prime Minister

*

Americans can eat garbage, provided you sprinkle it
liberally with ketchup, mustard, chilli sauce, Tabasco
sauce, cayenne pepper, or any other condiment which
destroys the original flavour of the dish.
Henry Miller, US novelist and critic

Boy, those French: they have a different word
for everything!
Steve Martin, US film actor

Imagine the Lord talking French! Aside from a few
odd words in Hebrew, I took it completely for granted
that God had never spoken anything but the most
dignified English.
CLARENCE SHEPARD DAY, US writer

*

Food isolates the French almost as much as their
language. That would not be serious if France were at
least certain of remaining a refuge for good food.
THEODORE ZELDIN, British historian

*

Never criticize Americans.
They have the best taste that money can buy.
MILES KINGTON, British writer and journalist

*

The Englishman who has lost his fortune
is said to have died of a broken heart.
RALPH WALDO EMERSON, US poet and essayist

*

German is the most extravagantly ugly language –
it sounds like someone using a sick bag on a 747.
WILLY RUSHTON, British comedian

Nation Shall Speak Insults Unto Nation

A Frenchman must be always talking, whether he knows
anything of the matter or not; an Englishman is content
to say nothing, when he has nothing to say.
Samuel Johnson,
British lexicographer, critic and essayist

✻

I hate the French because they are all slaves,
and wear wooden shoes.
Oliver Goldsmith, Irish-born British novelist,
playwright and poet

✻

In our country we have those three unspeakably
precious things: freedom of speech, freedom
of conscience, and the prudence to never practise
either of them.
Mark Twain, US writer (about America)

✻

Germany – the diseased world's bathhouse.
Mark Twain

✻

In Paris they simply stared when I spoke to them in
French; I never did succeed in making those idiots
understand their own language.
Mark Twain

✻

I can speak French, but I cannot understand it.
Mark Twain

The problem with Ireland is that it's a country full
of genius, but with absolutely no talent.
HUGH LEONARD, Irish writer and playwright

*

The French are sawed-off sissies who eat snails and slugs
and cheese that smells like people's feet. Utter cowards
who force their own children to drink wine, they gibber
like baboons even when you try to speak to them
in their own wimpy language.
P. J. O'ROURKE, US satirist and journalist

*

You can always reason with a German. You can always
reason with a barnyard animal, too, for all the good it does.
P. J. O'ROURKE

*

The Greeks – dirty and impoverished descendants
of a bunch of la-de-da fruit salads who invented
democracy and then forgot how to use it while
walking around dressed up as girls.
P. J. O'ROURKE

France is a country where the money falls apart,
but you can't tear the toilet paper.
BILLY WILDER, Austrian-born
US film director, writer and producer

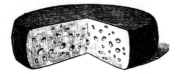

The French will only be united under the threat
of danger. Nobody can simply bring together a country
that has 265 kinds of cheese.
Charles de Gaulle,
French President, soldier and statesman

*

The best thing I know between France and England
is the sea.
Douglas Jerrold, British writer

*

The German mind has a talent for making no mistakes
but the very greatest.
Clifton Fadiman, US intellectual and author

*

This is one race of people for whom psychoanalysis
is of no use whatsoever.
Sigmund Freud, Austrian physician
and founder of psychoanalysis (said of the Irish)

*

No one ever went broke underestimating the taste
of the American public.
H. L. Mencken, US journalist, critic and editor

[127]

The Japanese have perfected good manners and made them indistinguishable from rudeness.
PAUL THEROUX, US travel writer and novelist

*

Russians will consume marinated mushrooms and vodka, salted herring and vodka, smoked salmon and vodka, salami and vodka, caviar on brown bread and vodka, pickled cucumbers and vodka, cold tongue and vodka, red beet salad and vodka, scallions and vodka – anything and everything and vodka.
HEDRICK SMITH, US journalist

*

Scotland: a land of meanness, sophistry and lust.
LORD BYRON, British poet

The food in Yugoslavia is fine if you like pork tartare.
ED BEGLEY JNR,
US TV and film actor

*

All Englishmen talk as if they've got a bushel of plums stuck in their throats, and then, after swallowing them, get constipated from the pits.
W. C. FIELDS, US actor and comedian

The Information Superbollocks, or Why were morons ever allowed on the Internet?

'A world awash in information is one in which information has very little market value.'
PAUL KRUGMAN, US economist

Information superhighway? Hah! Whatever the information is, it certainly isn't 'super'. Not the sort of guff you get on the Internet, anyhow. When it was made available to all and sundry several years ago, it promised us so much: shopping online, research, lots to read and do and see, but look at the rubbish that's there – taking up precious bandwidth (or whatever it's called). A random trawl came up with a few websites that make you wonder why their owners haven't got something better to do. It's enough to make you want to rip your typing fingers off, one by one.

There's a webcat, apparently, that 'sits on your screen and interacts with your mouse'. What's the point of that? And while we're on the subject of annoying things to do with computers, Microsoft has produced something called Clippit, which is a maddeningly grovelling little paperclip-shaped icon that sits with an inane smile on its face, waiting for you to make a mistake. As soon as you do, it pounces and throws up a totally distracting yellow note on your screen saying, 'It looks as if you're about to write a letter. Do you need some help?' No, you exasperating electronic moron, I know how to write letters, thank you very much. Then there's Zippotricks: 'See 320 cool tricks to do with your Zippo lighter.' Next!

There's a site devoted to pictures of stuff that's been left on the pavement. Among these treasured pics are shots of a prosthetic leg and an inflated rubber glove. Just think how deprived you would be if you never happen across this website.

Another site offers you a pet rock. No, not a rockfish or a roc – that large mythical bird from the Arabian Nights – but a heavy bit of hard mineral aggregate. *That* type of rock. The sort of thing you often feel like throwing at your screen, hoping that it magically traverses the superhighway and hits the website owner right between the eyes. How sad would you have to be to buy one of these supremely useless objects?

When you've finished having a Socratic discourse with your pet rock, you can go to a site devoted to practising origami with toilet paper; or you can be a total sicko and visit a site devoted to plane crashes. 'Name That Beard' is a site that lets you – well, name that beard. You look at a beard and decide whether it belongs to Karl Marx, the Archbishop of Canterbury or Rolf Harris. You can also 'Ask Satan' a question or match beer bottles to their labels, and there's a site that teaches you how to play air guitar . . .

Quotations about the Internet are few and far between. In fact, so few and far between that what few *are* to be found are all crap and aren't worth bothering with. Anyway, similar sentiments are to be found among those who moan about technology in general (see the 'White Heat and Snake Oil' chapter).

But there is one, and it was penned by Andy, co-author of this book. It just came to him one day when he was ironing the cat:

> A world once served by gods and heroes
> Now gets by with ones and zeros.

Not bad, even though he does say so himself. But, then, he would.

However, give it ten or twenty years, and there'll be an entire *Oxford Guide to Quotations About the Internet from Grumpy Gits Who Still Live in the World of Inkwells, Blotting Paper and Basildon Bond* – a guaranteed bestseller, surely?

Battles of the Sexes, or What is it about men and women that makes them bitch at one another?

> 'I believe in tying the marriage knot,
> as long as it's around the woman's neck.'
> W. C. FIELDS, US actor and comedian

What is it about men and women (usually when they've entered coupledom) that they have to be so damned bitchy about? Why can't they just live in harmony?

Perhaps the best solution would be if all couples were of the same-sex variety . . . Until this happens, though, the relentless rowing between husbands and wives, boyfriends and girlfriends, is destined to go on and on and on . . .

There are theories about why men are grumpier than women. There are also theories about why the opposite is apparently true. In 2002, some scientists came up with an explanation for the former, with the conclusion that men were suffering from 'irritable-male syndrome'. It amounts, they said, to a fall-off in a middle-aged man's levels of the male hormone testosterone, which duly affects their brains and therefore their behaviour. So a conversation like this might be quite commonplace nowadays:

'You're a grumpy bugger, you are.'
'No, I'm not.'
'Yes, you are.'
'No, I'm not. My testosterone levels are a bit on the low side today, that's all. It's scientific. Now sod off!'

In the resulting report, Gerald Lincoln of the Medical Research Council's Human Reproductive Sciences Unit in Edinburgh revealed that he thought stress can cause men of *any* age to suffer a fall in testosterone levels, affecting their mood and behaviour, which means that in theory it's quite possible to develop into a miserable old git even if you're only twenty-three.

Lincoln's work was featured in *New Scientist*, where it was reported that he first identified irritable-male syndrome in Soay sheep (these are the little brown ones found in the Outer Hebrides). As rams' testosterone levels fell off during the winter, they were much more likely to get really crotchety and lash out with their horns.

Now for the women. A piece by Victor Lewis Smith in *The Times* in April 2005 reported that it was they, and not men, who were the grumpier sex. 'Far from following the lead of Victor Meldrew,' he writes, 'elderly men are calm old buffers who refuse to fly off the handle. Their womenfolk, on the other hand, have been boiling with anger since they were young, a situation that fails to improve with age.'

He quotes Jane Barnett of Middlesex University as saying that Victor Meldrew – the grumpy old malcontent in the BBC sitcom *One Foot in the Grave* – was the exception. According to Smith, she said that the *Grumpy Old Women* television programme, featuring a selection of ranting women such as Janet Street-Porter and Germaine Greer, who vented their collective spleen at a succession of irritants, was far better at reflecting reality than its counterpart, *Grumpy Old Men*.

Barnett was presenting a talk on anger to the British Psychological Society, and her studies, she said, revealed that, on the whole, women showed their anger more than men. They displayed the same amount of crotchetiness in the 18–25 age range, but then this commendable characteristic diverged between men and women. As they approach their fortieth birthday, men are far less prone to anger than women, whose anger levels remain the same throughout their lives.

Now there's something to ponder on, chaps. But the good news for you ladies is that if your old man's giving you grief, you can administer a swift knee to the knackers and blame it on your grumpiness gene.

Sometimes in good humour and sometimes in malice, the two sexes have had a fair few things to say about each other over the ages . . .

Quotable Querulous Quibbles About the Sexes

Men are those creatures with two legs
and eight hands.
JAYNE MANSFIELD, US film actress

*

And a woman is only a woman,
but a good cigar is a smoke.
RUDYARD KIPLING, British writer and poet

Male, *n.*: a member of the unconsidered, or negligible, sex. The male of the human race is commonly known to the female as Mere Man. The genus has two varieties: good providers and bad providers.
Ambrose Bierce,
US writer and journalist

*

Marriage – the most advanced form of warfare
in the modern world.
Malcolm Bradbury, British writer

*

All marriages are happy. It's the living together afterward
that causes all the trouble.
Raymond Hull,
British-born Canadian writer

*

A woman will lie about anything, just to stay in practice.
Philip Marlowe, US novelist

*

Though marriage makes man and wife one flesh,
it leaves 'em still two fools.
William Congreve, British playwright

*

There are no great men, buster. There are only men.
Charles Schnee, US screenwriter,
from his 1952 screenplay *The Bad and the Beautiful*

A good marriage would be between a blind wife
and a deaf husband.
MICHEL DE MONTAIGNE, French essayist

Some of my best leading men have been dogs and horses.
ELIZABETH TAYLOR, US actress

*

Her arms are too fat, her legs are too short,
and she is too big in the bust.
RICHARD BURTON, Welsh actor,
on his new wife Elizabeth Taylor

*

The secret of a happy marriage remains a secret.
HENNY YOUNGMAN, British-born
US comedian and actor

*

There is one woman whom fate has destined
for each of us. If we miss her we are saved.
ANONYMOUS

*

Women want mediocre men, and men are working hard
to become as mediocre as possible.
MARGARET MEAD, US anthropologist

Marriage is the price men pay for sex; sex is the price
women pay for marriage.
ANONYMOUS

✳

Boys will be boys, and so will a lot of middle-aged men.
KIN HUBBARD, US humorist

✳

Wedding rings: the world's smallest handcuffs.
ANONYMOUS

✳

Marriage is an arrangement by which two people
start by getting the best out of each other
and often end by getting the worst.
GERALD BRENAN, British writer

✳

The more I see of men, the more I admire dogs.
MADAME ROLAND, French writer (attributed)

It was very good of God to let Carlyle
and Mrs Carlyle marry one another,
and so make two people miserable instead of four.
SAMUEL BUTLER, British writer

*

Brigands demand your money or your life; women
require both.
SAMUEL BUTLER

*

Bigamy is having one husband too many,
monogamy is the same.
Quoted as an epigraph to ERICA JONG's *Fear of Flying*

*

Once a woman gives you her heart,
you can never get rid of the rest of her body.
JOHN VANBRUGH, British architect and playwright

*

Sometimes I wonder if men and women really suit
each other. Perhaps they should live next door
and just visit now and then.
KATHARINE HEPBURN, US actress

*

A woman's preaching is like a dog's walking
on his hinder legs. It is not done well;
but you are surprised to find it done at all.
SAMUEL JOHNSON, British lexicographer, critic
and essayist, quoted by his biographer JAMES BOSWELL

When a man steals your wife, there is no better revenge
than to let him keep her.
SACHA GUITRY, French writer

*

Love is the delusion that one woman
differs from another.
H. L. MENCKEN,
US journalist, critic and editor

*

The chief reason why marriage is rarely a success
is that it is contracted while the partners are insane.
JOSEPH COLLINS, US writer

*

Spouse: someone who'll stand by you through all the
trouble you wouldn't have had if you'd stayed single.
ANONYMOUS

A woman needs a man like a fish needs a bicycle.
FEMINIST SLOGAN, 1970s

*

The only time a woman really succeeds in changing
a man is when he is a baby.
NATALIE WOOD, US actress

*

A man's worst difficulties begin
when he is able to do as he likes.
T. H. HUXLEY, British scientist

*

The trouble with Ian [Fleming] is that he gets off
with women because he can't get on with them.
ROSAMOND LEHMANN, British novelist

*

Marriage is a great institution,
but I'm not ready for an institution.
MAE WEST, US actress

*

There is no fury like an ex-wife searching for a new lover.
CYRIL CONNOLLY,
British writer and critic

*

If you catch a man, throw him back.
WOMEN'S LIB SLOGAN, 1970s

Are You a Miserable Old Git?

Outside every thin girl is a fat man, trying to get in.
KATHARINE WHITEHORN,
British journalist and writer

✳

Many a man has fallen in love with a girl in a light
so dim he would not have chosen a suit by it.
MAURICE CHEVALIER, French actor

✳

My wife and I tried to breakfast together,
but we had to stop or our marriage would
have been wrecked.
WINSTON CHURCHILL,
British Prime Minister

✳

A wedding is just like a funeral
except that you get to smell your own flowers.
GRACE HANSEN

✳

I have nothing against women – after all,
it was a woman who drove me to drink,
and I've never written to thank her for it.
W. C. FIELDS,
US actor and comedian

✳

Women are like elephants to me: nice to look at,
but I wouldn't want to own one.
W. C. FIELDS

BATTLES OF THE SEXES

Love matches are made by people who are content,
for a month of honey, to condemn themselves
to a life of vinegar.
MARGUERITE, COUNTESS OF BLESSINGTON,
Irish writer

*

I bequeathe all my property to my wife,
on condition that she remarry immediately.
Then there will be at least one man to regret my death.
HEINRICH HEINE,
German poet (in his will)

*

I never knew what real happiness was until I got married.
And by then it was too late.
MAX KAUFFMAN

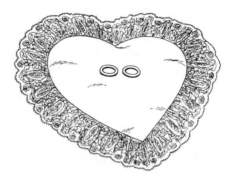

A woman's mind is cleaner than a man's.
She changes it more often.
OLIVER HERFORD,
US author and illustrator

✳

Love, *n*.: a temporary insanity curable by marriage.

Marriage, *n*.: the state or condition of a community
consisting of a master, a mistress and two slaves,
making in all, two.
AMBROSE BIERCE, US writer and journalist

✳

The old woman was not only ugly with the ugliness
age brings us all but showed signs of formidable ugliness
by birth – pickle-jar chin, mainsail ears and a nose
like a trigonometry problem. What's more,
she had the deep frown and snit wrinkles
that come from a lifetime of bad character.
P. J. O'ROURKE,
US satirist and journalist

Marriage is give and take. You'd better give it to her,
or she'll take it anyway.
JOEY ADAMS, US humorist

*

The one charm of marriage is that it makes a life
of deception absolutely necessary for both parties.
OSCAR WILDE, Irish playwright and poet
(from *The Picture of Dorian Gray*)

*

I sometimes think that God, in creating man,
somewhat overestimated His ability.
OSCAR WILDE

*

Rich bachelors should be heavily taxed. It is not fair
that some men should be happier than others.
OSCAR WILDE

Women's intuition is the result of millions of years
of not thinking.
RUPERT HUGHES, US author

*

My husband and I divorced over religious differences.
He thought he was God, and I didn't.
ANONYMOUS

*

All husbands are alike, but they have different faces
so you can tell them apart.
ANONYMOUS

*

Marriage is a romance in which the hero dies
in the first chapter.
ANONYMOUS

*

You have two choices in life: You can stay single and be
miserable, or get married and wish you were dead.
ANONYMOUS

Rantings of a Miserable Old Git: Part IV

DENTISTS' DRILLS: Now why, in the name of all that's humane, hasn't somebody invented a dentist's drill that doesn't go *zzzzeeeeeeeeeee, zzzzeeeeeeeeeee?* Better still, it's been reported that scientists are trying to develop ways of treating cavities without the use of drills. Well, why don't they get on with it?

DANDRUFF: Other people's, usually. And these dandruff-ridden folk are always sitting in front of you on buses, and you're having to keep a beady eye on your kneecaps for any stray flakes of dandruff that fall off the shoulders of their coats and drop on you delicately. Ugh! *They* might be happy to have shoulders that look as if Mount Etna's just had another cough and flung a ton of ash all over the place, but innocent bystandders or fellow travellers are definitely not.

MAPS: Not only can you never fold the damn things back again, the place you want to be is always right in the crease of the most folded bit. As for those silly things in the middle of town centres that tell you, 'You are here', how do they know? You didn't *tell* them you were coming.

THREE-THIRTY IN THE MORNING: Whenever you have one of those dark nights of the soul, this is the time you experience it – all at once. You wake up at 3.30 in the morning, in a sweat, as, almost palpably, your self-awareness crashes into your skull as though downloaded from a celestial server: you recall who you are, where you are and at what point in your life you are; you acknowledge your mortality, your debts and your guilt at whatever it was you did last night and throughout all your life so far; you tally your failures, your low moments, and are horrified at the thought that they'll continue for the rest of your life, which you suddenly wish would end right now, if only you'd got all your affairs in order, which you haven't. You do whatever you normally do to try to get back to sleep, and invariably fail. Yep, 3.30 a.m. should be banished from the clock face by international agreement.

FLIES: They refuse to go away. *Bzz, bzz.* You go *swat, swat.* And they just go *bzz, bzz.* They land on your butter knife or the rim of your beer glass or wine glass. *Bzz, bzz.* And do you know what the disgusting creatures do once they land? They throw up, that's what they do. No manners. What they're actually doing is upchucking digestive enzymes to liquefy food. And they have 1,500 taste hairs on their feet, so they've already decided the rim of your cup or your cutlery is going to yield some goodies. Anyway, you decide fly paper is hideous and don't wish to spray poisons about the place, so you put one of those ultraviolet fly zappers up in your kitchen, and they *bzz, bzz* to the other end of the room and make a nuisance of themselves there. Here's a secret. They have compound eyes, so can see you coming with that rolled-up copy of *The Sunday Times.* It sees your movements and it's off. *Bzz, bzz.* But approach very, very slowly. They can detect movement only down to a certain speed, you see. Bang! *Bzz, splat!* You've got him.

Boom, boom: Not the catchphrase of Basil Brush, but total brain-deads who are so generous of spirit that they want you to share their music with them wherever they go – so much so that they allow you to be deafened by the bass from their ultra-mega super-duper ear-shredder extra-woofer new ThunderSound™ Shatterblaster™ speaker system, which is using their car's own structure as an amplifier to make it more ultra, more mega, more super, more sodding duper, and adding an extra dimension of wooferistic megabass banality. And they very likely have the speakers in the doors. Do these thoughtless idiots realize they run the risk of going deaf by the time they turn thirty?

Call centres: First, it's the seemingly endless menu. 'You have six options.' You select one. 'You now have eight more options.' You swear under your breath and select one. 'Please select from the following five options.' You swear some more, louder this time, jump up and down a bit, then select an option. 'If your mother has a maiden name, please select 1.' Despair begins to darken your very soul. You hang up, take a deep breath, count to ten and throw the phone out of the nearest open window.

Blackboards and fingernails: No need even to explain this one. Just putting those two words within a gnat's knacker of each other has got your teeth on edge and sent a shiver running down your spine.

Oh Come, All Ye Morons, or 'Tis the season to be grouchy

"'Bah," said Scrooge. "Humbug!'"
CHARLES DICKENS (from *A Christmas Carol*)

∗

It's that time again. Sickly coloured lights camp up the streets; carols and other jolly tosh are spilling out from loudspeakers in stores; shelves are bristling with wrapping paper in festively garish colours; you can't buy what you want to buy because everything on sale is seasonal; ads on TV show morons wearing paper hats, partying; people who don't drink at other times of the year fall out of pubs, rat-arsed, unable to hold their beer. Yes, it's that time again: September.

It gets earlier every year. But how long will it be before *next* Christmas is joined onto the end of *this* Christmas? There should be a law against it. And it's all the fault of the shops and the multi-mega-supermarkets. If it weren't for companies' obsessions with filling your home with tat and crap, there'd be a nice respectable eleven-month gap between this Christmas and next.

In the old days you looked forward to the special, joyous few weeks when the anticipation kicked in, then Christmas Eve arrived, followed by the day itself, then the wind-down with a bit of partying on New Year's Eve to bid the season *au revoir* for another year. But in modern times, how can you enjoy it now that it's virtually all year round? We've all been robbed of our childhood, thanks to the money-grabbing marketing men. Ebenezer Scrooge had it about right: humbug. (We once asked our local pub to put small plates of free humbugs on the bar. Bar humbugs. They didn't get the joke, miserable old gits.)

Though Christmas is traditionally a time for family get-togethers, sometimes you wish you'd never bothered. Tensions invariably run high, long-held grudges rear their ugly head once the demon drink starts flowing, and before you know it you've got a familial disagreement of civil-war proportions on your hands. Peace and goodwill to all men? Hardly.

There are other annual events that turn people into utter prats. You go down the street and that dizzy woman from Number 43 has adorned the outside of her house with bunting and balloons because her twit of a husband has reached his fortieth birthday and she thinks it's a really, really good idea to tell the entire street about it. Oh, jolly good for him, you don't say as you think grouchily, 'She's a moron for doing it and he's a *total* moron for letting her.'

Then there are the annual holidays, when all the lemmings swamp the motorways and departure lounges, complaining about how crowded everything is and failing spectacularly to realize that *they* are the ones contributing to the problem. Idiots. Off they go, blow a year's savings on getting pissed on overpriced concoctions they've never tried before or even ever heard of, and they come back with skin the colour of boot polish and think it's an achievement that they've got a tan.

But what is it about the British and the way they enjoy themselves? We must be the laughing stock of the entire world. The aforementioned suntan is enough to give us malignant melanomas, we pack ourselves into pubs and bars in the long drawn-out approach to Christmas, and we fork out huge amounts of our hard-earned cash to come back and complain about the roads/ airport/hotel/waiters/poolside-grabbing Germans/ other foreigners/the food (delete as applicable).

From Christmas and New Year to birthday celebrations and holidays, sometimes you're better off staying at home. But we won't go on about it, and instead offer some alternative points of view.

Quotable Querulous Quibbles About Special Occasions

Why for fifty-three years I've put up with it now!
I MUST stop Christmas from coming! . . . But HOW?
DR SEUSS, US writer and illustrator
(said by the Grinch in *How The Grinch Stole Christmas*)

*

After all, what are birthdays?
Here today and gone tomorrow.
EEYORE (from A. A. Milne's
The House at Pooh Corner)

Oh Come, All Ye Morons

In England you worship two goddesses: one is Christmas, the other one is holidays. As soon as they finish advertising for Christmas on television and in the papers, the next big thing is the annual holiday.

Buchi Emecheta,
Nigerian novelist and publisher

*

He . . . threw them about the room saying: 'We always smash our Christmas presents straight away; we don't want any.' Smashing his toys thus stood in his unconscious for smashing his father's genitals. During this first hour he did in fact break several toys.

Melanie Klein, Austrian psychoanalyst

*

Darkness is cheap, and Scrooge liked it.

Charles Dickens, British novelist
(from *A Christmas Carol*)

*

'Merry Christmas! Out upon merry Christmas! What's Christmas time to you but a time for paying bills without money; a time for finding yourself a year older, but not an hour richer; a time for balancing your books and having every item in 'em through a round dozen of months presented dead against you? If I could work my will,' said Scrooge indignantly, 'every idiot who goes about with "Merry Christmas" on his lips, should be boiled with his own pudding, and buried with a stake of holly through his heart. He should!'

Charles Dickens (from *A Christmas Carol*)

The Wit of Being a Miserable Old Git, or How to be moody and funny at the same time

Just because you spend most of your life in a state of doom and gloom, and you've barely got a good word to say about anybody or anything, it doesn't mean your negative attitude and observations shouldn't raise a few laughs at the same time.

A great many successful comedians have made a career out of being a humorous old grump (W. C. Fields and Groucho Marx, for example), so why not follow their lead? A cutting criticism or a rude riposte uttered by a cranky curmudgeon can be a source of great amusement to observers, albeit at the expense of the unfortunate subject of the remark. So to bring this miserable tome to a fitting end, read and learn from the mirthmaking masters of moodiness:

Putting down politicians

I have seen better-looking faces on pirate flags.
ANONYMOUS remark made about
British Prime Minister Sir Alec Douglas-Home

It has been a political career of this man to begin
with hypocrisy, proceed with arrogance,
and to finish with contempt.
THOMAS PAINE, British political writer,
on US President John Adams

*

He is undoubtedly living proof that a pig's bladder
on a stick can be elected as a Member of Parliament.
TONY BANKS, British politician,
on fellow MP Terry Dicks

*

Gerry Ford is so dumb that he can't fart
and chew gum at the same time.
LYNDON B. JOHNSON, US President, on fellow
US politician (and later President) Gerald Ford

*

Major is what he is: a man from nowhere, going nowhere,
heading for a well-merited obscurity as fast as his
mediocre talents can carry him.
PAUL JOHNSON, British journalist,
on British Prime Minister John Major

*

Malcolm Fraser could be described as a cutlery man – he
was born with a silver spoon in his mouth and he uses it
to stab his colleagues in the back.
BOB HAWKE, Australian trade-union leader
(later Prime Minister), referring to the then
Australian Prime Minister

Are You a Miserable Old Git?

Richard Nixon is a no-good lying bastard.
He can lie out of both sides of his mouth at the same
time, and if he ever caught himself telling the truth
he'd lie just to keep his hand in.
HARRY S. TRUMAN, 33rd US President,
referring to the man who would become
37th US President, Richard Nixon

*

A modest little man with much to be modest about.
WINSTON CHURCHILL, former British Prime Minister,
on his successor Clement Attlee

Whenever Stafford has tried to increase the sum
of human happiness, grass never grows again.
ANONYMOUS remark made about British politician
Sir Stafford Cripps

*

A political leader worthy of assassination.
IRVING LAYTON, Canadian writer,
on Canadian Prime Minister Pierre Trudeau

Of all the men, whom it was ever my lot to accost and
to waste civilities upon, Adams was the most doggedly
and systematically repulsive. With a vinegar aspect,
cotton in his leathern ears, and hatred of England
in his heart, he sat in the frivolous assemblies
of Petersburg like a bulldog among spaniels.
W. H. Lyttelton, British writer,
on 6th US President John Quincy Adams

*

As an intellectual, he bestowed upon the games
of golf and bridge all the enthusiasm and perseverance
that he withheld from books and ideas.
Emmet John Hughes, US writer,
on US President Dwight D. Eisenhower

*

The word 'honour' in the mouth of Mr Webster
is like the word 'love' in the mouth of a whore.
Ralph Waldo Emerson, US essayist,
on US politician Daniel Webster

*

Government: a kind of legalized pillage.
Kin Hubbard, US humorist

*

When they circumcised Herbert Samuel,
they threw away the wrong bit.
Attributed to David Lloyd George,
British Prime Minister, on fellow British politician
Herbert Samuel

Are You a Miserable Old Git?

He sailed through American history like a steel ship
loaded with monoliths of granite.
H. L. Mencken,
US journalist and critic
on US President Grover Cleveland

*

A tin-horn politician with the manner of a rural corn
doctor and the mien of a ham actor.
H. L. Mencken
on US President Warren G. Harding

*

A good politician is as unthinkable as an honest burglar.
H. L. Mencken

*

Randolph Churchill went into hospital . . . to have a lung
removed. It was announced that the trouble was not
'malignant' . . . I remarked that it was a typical triumph
of modern science to find the only part of Randolph
that was not malignant and remove it.
Evelyn Waugh,
British writer (in his diary)

*

His temper, naturally morose, has become licentiously
peevish. Crossed in his Cabinet, he insults the House
of Lords and plagues the most eminent of his colleagues
with the crabbed malice of a maundering witch.
Benjamin Disraeli, former British Prime Minister,
on fellow politician the Earl of Aberdeen

If Gladstone fell into the Thames that would be
a misfortune, and if anybody pulled him out that,
I suppose, would be a calamity.
Benjamin Disraeli
on British Prime Minister William Gladstone

On players from the world of film

She turned down the role of Helen Keller
because she couldn't remember the lines.
Joan Rivers, US comedian,
on US actress Bo Derek

*

If Greta really wants to be alone, she should come
to a performance of one of her films in Dublin.
Unknown Irish critic
on Swedish-born actress Greta Garbo

*

Working with her [Julie Andrews] is like being hit over
the head with a Valentine's card.
Christopher Plummer, Canadian actor

[159]

Are You a Miserable Old Git?

He looks as if his idea of fun would be to find
a cold damp grave and sit in it.
RICHARD WINNINGTON, US critic,
on US actor Paul Heinreid

*

He's the kind of guy who, if you say,
'Hiya, Clark, how are you?' is stuck for an answer.
AVA GARDNER, US actress,
on fellow US actor Clark Gable

*

She is uniquely suited to play
a woman of limited intelligence.
US film critics HARRY and MICHAEL MEDVED,
on US actress Farah Fawcett

*

As wholesome as a bowl of cornflakes,
and at least as sexy.
DWIGHT MACDONALD, US critic,
describing US actress Doris Day

*

Acting is like rollerskating: once you know how to do it,
it is neither stimulating nor exciting.
GEORGE SANDERS, British actor

*

A walking X-ray.
OSCAR LEVANT, US wit,
on US actress Audrey Hepburn

A man of many talents – all of them minor.
LESLIE HALLIWELL, British film historian,
on US film director Blake Edwards

∗

Overweight, overbosomed, overpaid and under-talented,
she set the acting profession back a decade.
DAVID SUSSKIND,
US producer and talk-show host,
on US actress Elizabeth Taylor

∗

She has only two expressions – joy and indigestion.
DOROTHY PARKER, US humorist, critic
and writer, on US actress Marion Davies

∗

To me, Edith looks like something
that would eat its young.
DOROTHY PARKER
on British actress Dame Edith Evans

∗

A vacuum with nipples.
OTTO PREMINGER, US film director,
on US actress Marilyn Monroe

ARE YOU A MISERABLE OLD GIT?

There are two kinds of directors in the theatre: those who think they are God, and those who are certain of it.
RHETTA HUGHES, US actress

✷

His features resembled a fossilized wash-rag.
ALAN BRIEN, British journalist,
on US actor Steve McQueen

✷

She has the face of an exhausted gnu,
the voice of an unstrung tennis racket,
and a figure of no describable shape.
JOHN SIMON, US critic,
on US actress Angelica Huston

An acting style that's really a nervous breakdown
in slow motion.
JOHN SIMON
on US actress Diane Keaton

✷

Diana Rigg is built like a brick mausoleum
with insufficient flying buttresses.
JOHN SIMON on British actress Diana Rigg

She looks like a cross between an aardvark
and an albino rat surmounted by a
platinum-coated horse bun.
John Simon on US singer and actress
Barbra Streisand

*

The biggest bug in the manure pile.
Elia Kazan, US film producer,
on fellow film producer Harry Cohn

*

Oh, excuse me. I thought you were a fellow
I once knew in Pittsburgh.
Groucho Marx to Greta Garbo,
having first removed her hat

Getting personal

A fat flabby little person with the face of a baker,
the clothes of a cobbler, the size of a barrelmaker,
the manners of a stocking salesman, and the dress
of an innkeeper.
Victor de Balabin, French writer,
on French novelist Honoré de Balzac

*

This arrogant, sour, ceremonial, pious,
chauvinistic egomaniac.
Elliot Gould, US actor,
on fellow actor and comedian Jerry Lewis

To be a moral thief, an unblushing liar,
a supreme dictator, and a cruel self-satisfied monster,
and attain, in the minds of millions, the status of a deity,
is not only remarkable, but a dismal reflection on
the human race. She had much in common with Hitler,
only no moustache.
Noël Coward, British playwright,
on the leader and founder of the Christian Science
movement, Mary Baker Eddy

*

The man was a major comedian, which is to say
that he had the compassion of an icicle, the effrontery
of a carnival shill and the generosity of a pawnbroker.
S. J. Perelman, US humorist,
on US comedian Groucho Marx

*

I never forget a face, but in your case
I'll be glad to make an exception.
Groucho Marx

*

I've had a perfectly wonderful evening.
But this wasn't it.
Groucho Marx
on leaving a dinner party

*

Dorothy Parker (to a friend who said that she would
not attend one of Parker's parties because she 'could not
bear fools'): 'Your mother could.'

Pearson is an infamous liar, a revolting liar,
a pusillanimous liar, a lying ass, a natural-born liar,
a liar by profession, a liar of living, a liar in the daytime,
a liar in the night-time, a dishonest, ignorant,
corrupt and grovelling crook.
Senator Kenneth McKellar,
on US journalist Drew Pearson

*

Englishwomen's shoes look as if they had been made
by someone who had often heard shoes described,
but who had never seen any.
Anonymous

*

I do not think that I shall ever forget the sight of
[Mount] Etna at sunset . . . Nothing I have ever seen
in Art or Nature was quite so revolting.
Evelyn Waugh, British writer (in his diary)

A tub of pork and beer.
Hector Berlioz, French composer,
on German-born composer George Frederick Handel

That grand imposter, that loathsome hypocrite,
that detestable traitor . . . that landscape of iniquity,
that sink of sin, that compendium of baseness,
who now calls himself our Protector.
The colourful views of ENGLISH ANABAPTISTS
on Lord Protector Oliver Cromwell

*

A woman whose face looked as if it had been made
of sugar and someone had licked it.
GEORGE BERNARD SHAW, Irish dramatist
and writer, on US dancer Isadora Duncan

*

Mr Dalton's aspect and manner were repulsive.
There was no gracefulness belonging to him.
His voice was harsh and brawling, his gait stiff
and awkward; his style of writing and conversation
dry and almost crabbed.
HUMPHRY DAVY, British chemist,
on fellow scientist John Dalton

On musicians and composers

The Beatles are not merely awful, I would consider it
sacrilegious to say anything less than that they are god-
awful. They are so unbelievably horrible, so appallingly
unmusical, so dogmatically insensitive to the magic of art,
that they qualify as crowned heads of anti-music . . .
WILLIAM F. BUCKLEY JNR,
US author and commentator

Mr Jones is, in the words of his own hit, not unusual . . .
at least not as a singer; as a sex symbol he is nothing short
of inexplicable.
Sheridan Morley, British critic,
on Welsh singer Tom Jones

*

All legs and hair with a mouth that could swallow
the whole stadium and the hot-dog stand.
Laura Lee Davies, British music critic,
on US singer Tina Turner

*

Listening to the Fifth Symphony of Ralph Vaughan
Williams is like staring at a cow for forty-five minutes.
Aaron Copland, US composer,
on British composer Ralph Vaughan Williams

I love Wagner, but the music I prefer is that of a cat hung
up by its tail outside a window and trying to stick to the
panes of glass with its claws.
Charles Baudelaire, French poet,
on German composer Richard Wagner

Stravinsky looks like a man who was potty-trained too
early, and that music proves it as far as I'm concerned.
Russell Hoban, British writer,
on Russian composer Igor Stravinsky

*

Composition indeed! Decomposition is the proper word
for such hated fungi, which choke up and poison the fertile
plains of harmony, threatening the world with drought.
A frank review of the work of Franz Liszt,
which appeared in *Musical World* in 1855

On dead people

The world is rid of Lord Byron,
but the deadly slime of his touch still remains.
John Constable, British painter,
shortly after the death of the British poet Byron

*

The reason so many people showed up at his funeral was
because they wanted to make sure he was dead.
Samuel Goldwyn, US film producer,
on the death of fellow producer Louis B. Mayer

On hearing the news that President Calvin Coolidge was
dead, US humorist, critic and writer Dorothy Parker
is alleged to have asked, 'How do they know?'

Jimmy Hoffa's most valuable contribution to the
American labour movement came at the moment
he stopped breathing on 3 July 1975.
DAN E. MOLDEA, US journalist,
on the unexplained disappearance
of US trade union leader Jimmy Hoffa

On writers and poets

Truman Capote has made lying an art.
A minor art.
GORE VIDAL, US writer

*

Shaw, most poisonous of all the poisonous haters of
England; despiser, distorter and denier of the plain truths
whereby men live; topsy-turvy perverter of all human
relationships; a menace to ordered social life;
irresponsible braggart, blaring self-trumpeter; idol
of opaque intellects and thwarted females; calculus
of contrariwise; flipperty-gibbet Pope of chaos;
portent and epitome of this generation's moral
and spiritual disorder.
HENRY A. JONES, British critic,
on Irish dramatist and writer George Bernard Shaw

*

An outstandingly unpleasant man, one who cheated
and stole from his friends and peed on their carpets.
KINGSLEY AMIS, British writer,
on Welsh poet Dylan Thomas

Are You a Miserable Old Git?

Reading Proust is like bathing
in someone else's dirty water.
ALEXANDER WOOLLCOTT, US writer,
on French novelist Marcel Proust

∗

I had thought that there could be only two worse writers
than Stephen Crane, namely two Stephen Cranes.
AMBROSE BIERCE, US writer

∗

His mind is so vile a mind, so cosy, hypocritical,
praise-mad, canting, envious, concupiscent.
SAMUEL TAYLOR COLERIDGE, British poet, critic
and philosopher, on British novelist Samuel Richardson

∗

A sycophant, a flatterer, a breaker of marriage vows,
a whining and inconstant person.
ELIZABETH FORSYTH, British writer,
on British playwright William Shakespeare

Henry James has a mind so fine
that no idea could violate it.
T. S. Eliot, US poet,
on US novelist Henry James

*

There are two ways of disliking poetry: one way is to
dislike it, the other is to read Pope.
Oscar Wilde on British poet Alexander Pope

*

As a writer he mastered everything except language, as a
novelist he can do everything except tell a story, as an
artist everything except articulate.
Oscar Wilde on British novelist George Meredith

*

Shaw is the most fraudulent, inept writer of Victorian
melodrama ever to gull a timid critic or fool a dull public.
John Osborne, British playwright,
on Irish dramatist and writer George Bernard Shaw

*

On the Road – that's not writing, that's typing.
Truman Capote, US writer,
on US novelist Jack Kerouac's best-known work

*

A disgusting common little man. He had never
been taught how to avoid being offensive.
Dame Rebecca West, British novelist,
on British writer Evelyn Waugh

Longfellow is to poetry
what the barrel-organ is to music.
VAN WYCK BROOKS, US critic,
on US poet Henry Wadsworth Longfellow

∗

So boring, you fall asleep halfway through her name.
ALAN BENNETT, British writer,
on Greek writer Arianna Stassinopoulos

∗

The first 200 pages of *Ulysses* – never have I read such
tosh. As for the first two chapters we will let them pass,
but the third, fourth, fifth, sixth – merely the scratchings
of pimples on the body of the bootboy at Claridge's.
VIRGINIA WOOLF, British novelist,
on Irish writer James Joyce's novel *Ulysses*

∗

He is limp and damp and milder
than the breath of a cow.
VIRGINIA WOOLF
on fellow British writer E. M. Forster

Shelley should not be read, but inhaled through a gas pipe.
Lionel Trilling, US critic,
on British poet Percy Bysshe Shelley

*

Thomas Gray walks as if he had fouled his small-clothes
and looks as if he smelt it.
Christopher Smart, British poet,
on fellow poet Thomas Gray

*

Gibbon is an ugly, affected, disgusting fellow,
and poisons our literary club for me. I class him
among infidel wasps and venomous insects.
James Boswell, Scottish writer and biographer,
on British historian Edward Gibbon (author of
The History of the Decline and Fall of the Roman Empire)

On monarchs

A pig, an ass, a dunghill, the spawn of an adder, a basilisk,
a lying buffoon, a mad fool with a frothy mouth.
Martin Luther, German Protestant theologian
and reformer, on Henry VIII

*

His intellect is of no more use than a pistol packed
in the bottom of a trunk if one were attacked
in the robber-infested Apennines.
Prince Albert, on his son the Prince of Wales,
later Edward VII

As just and merciful as Nero,
and as good a Christian as Mahomet.
JOHN WESLEY, British preacher,
on Queen Elizabeth I

Nowadays, a parlour-maid as ignorant
as Queen Victoria was when she came
to the throne would be classed as
mentally defective.
GEORGE BERNARD SHAW, Irish dramatist and writer

*

A more contemptible, cowardly, selfish, unfeeling dog
does not exist than this King . . . with vices and
weaknesses of the lowest and most contemptible order.
CHARLES GREVILLE, British diarist,
on King George IV

On artists

A decorator tainted with insanity.
KENYON COX, US critic,
on French painter Paul Gauguin

The last bit of methane left in the intestine
of the dead cow that is post-modernism.
ROBERT HUGHES, Australian art critic,
on US artist Jeff Koons

*

He bores me. He ought to have stuck
to his flying machines.
AUGUSTE RENOIR, French painter,
on Italian artist Leonardo da Vinci

Trading punches

NANCY ASTOR: Winston, if I were your wife I would
put poison in your coffee.
WINSTON CHURCHILL: Nancy, if I were your husband
I would drink it.

*

EARL OF SANDWICH: 'Pon my soul, Wilkes, I don't
know whether you'll die upon the gallows or of
the pox.
JOHN WILKES: That depends, my Lord, whether I
first embrace your Lordship's principles, or your
Lordship's mistresses.

*

THE MARQUESS OF LONDONDERRY: Have you read
my last book, Winston?
WINSTON CHURCHILL: No, I only read for pleasure
or for profit.

GEORGE BERNARD SHAW (*in a letter to Winston Churchill inviting him to the first night of his new play* St Joan):
Bring a friend – if you have one.

WINSTON CHURCHILL (*in his reply*): I cannot come. Would it be possible for you to let me have tickets for the second night – if there is one.

PAMELA HARRIMAN (*the British-born socialite and diplomat, ushering Dorothy Parker into a party ahead of her*):
Age before beauty.

DOROTHY PARKER: Pearls before swine.

Last word

I'm free of all prejudices. I hate everyone equally.
W. C. FIELDS, US actor and comedian